STARTUP
GUIDE

#startupeverywhere

Startup Guide Frankfurt

EDITORIAL
Publisher: Sissel Hansen
Editor: Marissa van Uden
Proofreader: Michelle Mills
Staff Writers: Charmaine Li, Shelley Pascual, L. Isaac Simon
Contributing Writers: Alexandra Connerty, Mark Fletcher, Tom Jackson, Rachel Gooby

PRODUCTION
Production Manager: Tim Rhodes
Project Manager: Eglė Duleckytė
Researchers: Pedro Ferreira, Lukas Lackinger, Hanna Yazdanfar

DESIGN & PHOTOGRAPHY
Designer: Cat Serafim
Photographers: Martin Liessl, Walter Vorjohann

Additional photography by Ryan Song, Christin Büttner, Alexander Heimann, Unsplash.com

Illustrations by Joana Carvalho, Cat Serafim
Photo Editor: Daniela Carducci

SALES & DISTRIBUTION
Global Partnerships Lead: Marlene do Vale marlene@startupguide.com
Business Developer - APAC and Africa: Anna Weissensteiner anna@startupguide.com
Startup Ecosystems Manager: Logan Ouellette logan@startupguide.com
Marketing Lead: İrem Topçuoğlu irem@startupguide.com

Printed in Berlin, Germany by
Medialis-Offsetdruck GmbH
Heidelbergerstraße 65, 12435 Berlin

Published by Startup Guide World IVS
Kanonbådsvej 2, 1437 Copenhagen K

info@startupguide.com
Visit us: startupguide.com
@StartupGuideHQ

Worldwide distribution by Die Gestalten
Visit: gestalten.com

ISBN: 978-3-947624-09-6

STARTUP GUIDE FRANKFURT

STARTUP GUIDE FRANKFURT

In partnership with **start** zero

Proudly supported by

SAP next-**gen** ⯈⯈

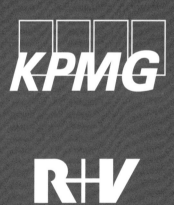 FrankfurtRheinMain GmbH
International Marketing of the Region

Sissel Hansen / Startup Guide

When people think about the Frankfurt region, the first thing that usually comes to mind is banks and glassy skyscrapers. Frankfurt, as a city, has always been known as a major financial hub in Europe, and now it's also rising in the ranks as a fintech hotspot. But it doesn't end there. The Frankfurt Rhine-Main region offers a lot more advantages for startups, many of which are often overlooked.

As the third largest metropolitan region in Germany, Frankfurt Rhine-Main covers parts of three federal states – Hessen, Rhineland-Palatinate and Bavaria – and is one of the strongest economic areas in Europe. There are large financial institutions, corporates and top-notch research universities sprinkled across the region in cities like Frankfurt, Darmstadt, Mainz, Offenbach and Wiesbaden. It's also worth mentioning that following the Brexit vote, the city of Frankfurt has become even more attractive to banks and bankers.

In addition to being a financial capital, Frankfurt Rhine-Main is home to a range of different industries, such as automotive, life sciences, chemical, industrial automation and logistics. Having large corporations like Software AG, Merck, Deutsche Bank and R+V Insurance in close proximity means that startups have many potential customers they can reach out to for partnerships.

Not only is it easy to get around within the region via public transport or car, traveling to other cities and countries is incredibly convenient by air or rail. The Frankfurt Airport is the busiest in Germany with more than three hundred destinations in ninety-one countries. It's no surprise to learn, then, that the Frankfurt Rhine-Main region is a magnet for people from around the world and has a big expat community.

Moreover, a number of organizations, such as TechQuartier (a community and workspace nurturing the development of entrepreneurs and innovators) and start zero (a platform that offers know-how and events for startups in different stages), have emerged in the past couple of years with the aim of strengthening the entrepreneurial ecosystem in the region. And the hard work seems to be paying off, because more and more startups are continuing to crop up in Frankfurt Rhine-Main.

We can't wait to explore the entrepreneurs, coworking spaces, accelerators, investors, schools and experts shaping the region's startup scene.

Sissel Hansen
Founder and CEO of Startup Guide

Peter Feldmann / Lord Mayor of Frankfurt am Main

Let me introduce you to Frankfurt Rhein-Main, the Central European region with a long tradition of successful entrepreneurs, where dynamic and innovative startups are finding a supportive and proactive infrastructure designed specifically for them. With the commitment of our partners, including C-suite leaders, academics, incubators, business accelerators and politicians, we have created a seamless corporate environment specifically designed to deliver tailored solutions and opportunities for startups and their founders.

As the economic powerhouse of Germany, our productivity is 20 percent above average and with strong clusters in IT, life sciences and automotive. We offer startups a broad customer base and supply chain to accelerate their growth. At our twenty-five universities and world-leading research institutes, around 250,000 students provide the future talent pool and technological innovations to support and increase our innovative power.

Frankfurt has long been recognized as the financial center of continental Europe, with strong resident banks and the Deutsche Börse offering ideal conditions for fintech companies. We operate the world's most important high-speed internet exchange, providing the backbone to our digital economy.

For my part, I would like to highlight our internationality as evidenced by the successful integration of citizens from over 180 nations, making it easy for global companies to settle here. With Germany's most important airport (and the best-connected within Europe), international business relationships can be built with ease. Finally, and most importantly, we are a region with an enviable quality of life, where a healthy work-life balance is possible and encouraged. Whilst offering an accessible cosmopolitan city culture, Frankfurt has outdoor recreation on its doorstep. Whether you prefer to stroll in fairy-tale forests, water-ski or visit wineries, all the activities and entertainment your family can imagine are right here.

Come and visit us and let us show you everything we can offer, and if you like what we can do for you and your company, we will help you expand into Frankfurt Rhine-Main and succeed.

I warmly invite you to become a part of Frankfurt's success.

Peter Feldmann,
Lord Mayor of Frankfurt am Main

Local Community Partner / start zero

Founding your startup in Frankfurt and the Rhein-Main region places you in the heart of Europe. With superb transport connections, other major cities like Paris, Berlin and London are within easy reach, making visiting investors or other startup hubs possible in a day.

There are over twenty universities in the region bursting with bright young talent that feeds the startup ecosystem, and we've seen a significant rise in the number of startups, incubators, accelerators, events and programs, driving innovation in business. Using the startup model is a unique way to improve, innovate and attract professionals from a broad range of industries. It's innovation like this that is transforming the Rhein-Main region and setting us apart from others.

Frankfurt is renowned as a banking city and for fintech, but many more startups are succeeding in other industries. One of the fastest-growing tech startups in Europe is based here. We have many other examples in areas such as real estate, pharmaceuticals, healthcare, automotive, logistics, AI and sports. Over the coming years, we expect to see more success stories, including more scale ups, acquisitions and unicorns. For this to happen, we have to ensure levels of investment continue to rise.

Frankfurt has an incredibly close-knit community, which supports and encourages growth from every angle. I am proud that start zero plays a role in that by connecting founders with mentors, speakers, tax advisors, lawyers, office spaces and investors. We couldn't do this without the support of our partners and we look forward to growing this further.

To get the most out of this guide, interact with it. Don't be afraid to connect and talk to the people and businesses featured. If you're an investor and a startup grabs your attention, reach out. If you are looking for a job, apply!

An ecosystem is only as strong as the community within it, so If you need guidance on the Rhein-Main ecosystem or would like to grow your idea to the next phase, please connect with us.

I'm looking forward to hearing from you.

Pedro Gonçalo Mota Ferreira,
Managing Director from start zero

contents

STARTUP
GUIDE
FRANKFURT

startups

programs

spaces

experts

founders

schools

investors

Local Ecosystem

[Facts & Figures]

- More than 70,000 people are employed in Frankfurt's financial institutions.
- Frankfurt is home to more than 200 foreign and domestic banks, including the European Central Bank, the Bundesbank and the German Stock Exchange.
- The top four growing subsectors are

  1. Advanced manufacturing and robotics (189% five-year increase in early-stage funding deals),

  2. Agtech and new food (171% five-year increase),

  3. Blockchain (163% five-year increase),

  4. Artificial intelligence, big data and analytics (77.5% five-year increase).

- A recent study by Accenture predicts that by 2035, the targeted use of AI will double the growth rate of the German economy to 3%.
- During the five years between 2012 and 2017, over 55% of all local VC investments were acquired by fintech startups.
- 8.5% of all startups in Frankfurt are in the artificial intelligence or big data and analytics subsector. This subsector has captured about 13% of all local VC investments in the past five years.
  360T's $800 million acquisition by Deutsche Börse is considered as the largest fintech exit of all time.

[Notable Startups]

- Acellere has created a software analytics platform called Gamma, which helps developers to identify and mitigate bugs and structural issues in software code. Founded by Sudarshan Bhide and Vishal Rai, Acellere recently raised a Series A round of €2.25 million.
- Antelope Club has developed a sportswear line of compression clothing with integrated electrodes that can be controlled via a smartphone app. Founded by Kay Rathschlag, Patrick Thumm and Philipp Schwarz, the company has raised $2.1 million to date.
- Founded in 2015, Covomo is an independent comparison portal for supplementary insurance products. Founders Simon Nörtersheuser and Eberhard Riesenkampff have raised $2.3 million in funding to date.
- CardioSecur provides mobile health services and products for people with cardiac issues, providing instant cardiac monitoring platforms and specializing in high-level twenty-two-lead ECG technology that provides a 360-degree view of the heart. The company recently closed a €5 million Series B financing led by KPN Ventures.

Sources: frankfurt-business.net, siliconrepublic.com, techobserver.org, rhein-main-startups.com

[City] # Frankfurt, Germany

[Statistics:] Area km²: 14,755
Population: 5.58 million
Companies: 407,000
GDP: US$247 billion

Intro to the City

Frankfurt, long known as a financial center, is increasingly becoming known as an international melting pot of culture, art, history and cuisine. While the pace of life is slower than in other cities, the startup scene is booming and it's fast-becoming the place to be. The city has a long tradition of trade due to its location in the heart of Europe. Trade fairs have been held in Frankfurt for over eight hundred years, and it continues to host fairs of international significance.

Winters are long, but when the sun shines, the city comes alive. Walk or cycle along the banks of the river Main, marvel at the skyscrapers or visit one of the many outdoor festivals. Explore Taunus, take a boat trip on the Rhein, visit historic castles or walk the RheinSteig, one of the most famous hiking trails in Germany. When it comes to museums and galleries, Frankfurt will not disappoint. The newly opened DomRömer Quarter offers a snapshot of history and stunning architecture. Here you'll find the Schirn, one of the most impressive contemporary galleries of its kind in Europe. The Städel Museum, located in the heart of the Museumsufer, boasts artwork spanning hundreds of years.

Frankfurters hold local traditions close to their hearts. Weekly markets showcase the best in local produce, and the *Kleinmarkthalle* (indoor market) is open every day for fresh groceries and international specialties. Gather there on a Saturday to enjoy locally-produced wine. *Grüne Soße* (green sauce) and *Apfelwein* (apple wine) are so well loved they have their own festivals in the spring.

Before You Come

Look to translate any official documents you need in advance, for example certificates of study or qualifications. This may help to speed up the process of registering in Germany and setting up your business. Learning some basic German phrases will go a long way and be appreciated more than you realize. If you're not an EU or EEA citizen, you'll need a valid visa before arriving in order to live and work in Germany. One of the biggest challenges you may face is finding accommodation. Competition is high in comparison to demand, so it's wise to start your search early. Start by researching the different residential areas online and ask questions on the Frankfurt Expats Facebook groups for advice from those who already live in Frankfurt. Being physically in the city will help you to secure a place, so short-term options like serviced apartments are a good starting point.

Cost of Living

Frankfurt is the second-most-expensive city to live in in Germany, but you can still live well, as you'll likely enjoy an above-average salary compared to the rest of Germany. Although taxes are high, the health and education systems are extremely good. Overall, you can have a great quality of life for less than in other areas in Europe. Your main outgoings will be for rent and health insurance, but public transport is reasonable and many museums are free to visit on the last Saturday of the month (search for "Satourday"). Dining out and socializing is as expensive as you make it; you can head to an Apfelwein Kneipe (a local pub serving apple wine) to eat and drink for less than €10, less than the price of a cocktail alone in a city center hotel bar. Alternatively, take a picnic to a park or visit one of the *Trinkhallen* (small convenience kiosks) that are becoming trendy places to meet.

Cultural Differences

Rest assured, the international vibe in Frankfurt creates the perfect blend of international and traditional German values. One German word that offers a great insight into German culture is *Feierabend*. There really is no direct translation, but it refers to the hours after you finish work and is an important time for unwinding. There is a strong distinction between work life and private life, and for some the two rarely mix.

Punctuality, orderliness and privacy are highly respected, and you'll notice this from the moment you arrive. Sunday is a sacred *Ruhetag* (quiet day), which can be quite a culture shock if you're used to living in the hustle and bustle of Paris or London. On Sundays, you won't find shops open for business, but cafes and restaurants are alive and buzzing, especially for brunch. Take the opportunity to go out and explore the surrounding areas (Taunus and the Rhein valley are only a short distance away).

Renting an Apartment

Rental prices vary greatly, with Westend, Nordend and Bornheim being the most expensive locations. Affordable housing exists, but you may have to persevere a little longer to find it. You can search for flat-shares (*Wohngemeinschaft* or *WG*) at **en.wg-suche.de.** For longer-term rentals, you'll need a bank account and a SCHUFA (credit rating) document, which you can get within three days online. Sign up on websites like **immobilienscout24.de** or **web. frankfurtrentals.de/en,** and be ready to act quickly. Expect to pay a deposit on your apartment, and be aware of the difference between "cold" rent (*Kaltmiete*) and "warm" rent (*Warmmiete*), which includes some utilities. Also find out if there's a kitchen; it's not uncommon to have to buy this separately. You'll need to register (*anmelden*) with your local citizen's office (*Bürgeramt*) within fourteen days of moving in. Take your ID and a completed *Wohnungsgeberbestätigung* (confirmation of residence) from your landlord. You'll then receive a *Meldebestätigung* (official registration document), which you'll need to keep safe.

See **Flats and Rentals** page **237**

Finding a Coworking Space

Frankfurt is fast becoming a hub for startups and small businesses. If you're new to the city, need motivation from others, or want to meet people to help grow your business, a coworking space can offer so much more than a desk. You can choose from some of the most stylish and trendy spaces, including WeWork, Mindspace, Beehive, and Social Impact Lab Frankfurt. Each coworking space has its own unique characteristics. Do you specialize in technology? Connect and network with relevant players at HUB31. Need to balance work and childcare? CoWorkPlay offers childcare services from 9 AM until 5 PM for children aged six months to three years. Book in some visits to see which one suits you best. Coworking spaces offer a range of membership plans, so do your research to find the one that's perfect for you. And keep an eye out for their events programs, which are also a great way to meet and connect with people.

See **Spaces** page **234**

Insurance

You can find insurance for every eventuality, but knowing which ones are mandatory for you personally and your business is essential. As a startup, you would benefit from getting advice from an insurance broker. Companies such as start zero or the IHK (Industrie- und Handelskammern or Chamber of Industry and Commerce) can help to put you in contact with the right people. Depending on whether you employ staff or have your own office or premises will determine what you need.

Health insurance in Germany is mandatory. There are various public and private insurance plans available, all of which offer a high standard of care. For private insurance, you must earn a certain gross salary (€59,400 in 2018) or be self-employed; otherwise you register for the state system. Home insurance isn't compulsory but is recommended to protect your belongings against flooding, fire or theft. If you own a car, you need to show that you have insurance before registering the vehicle.

See **Insurance Companies** page **237**

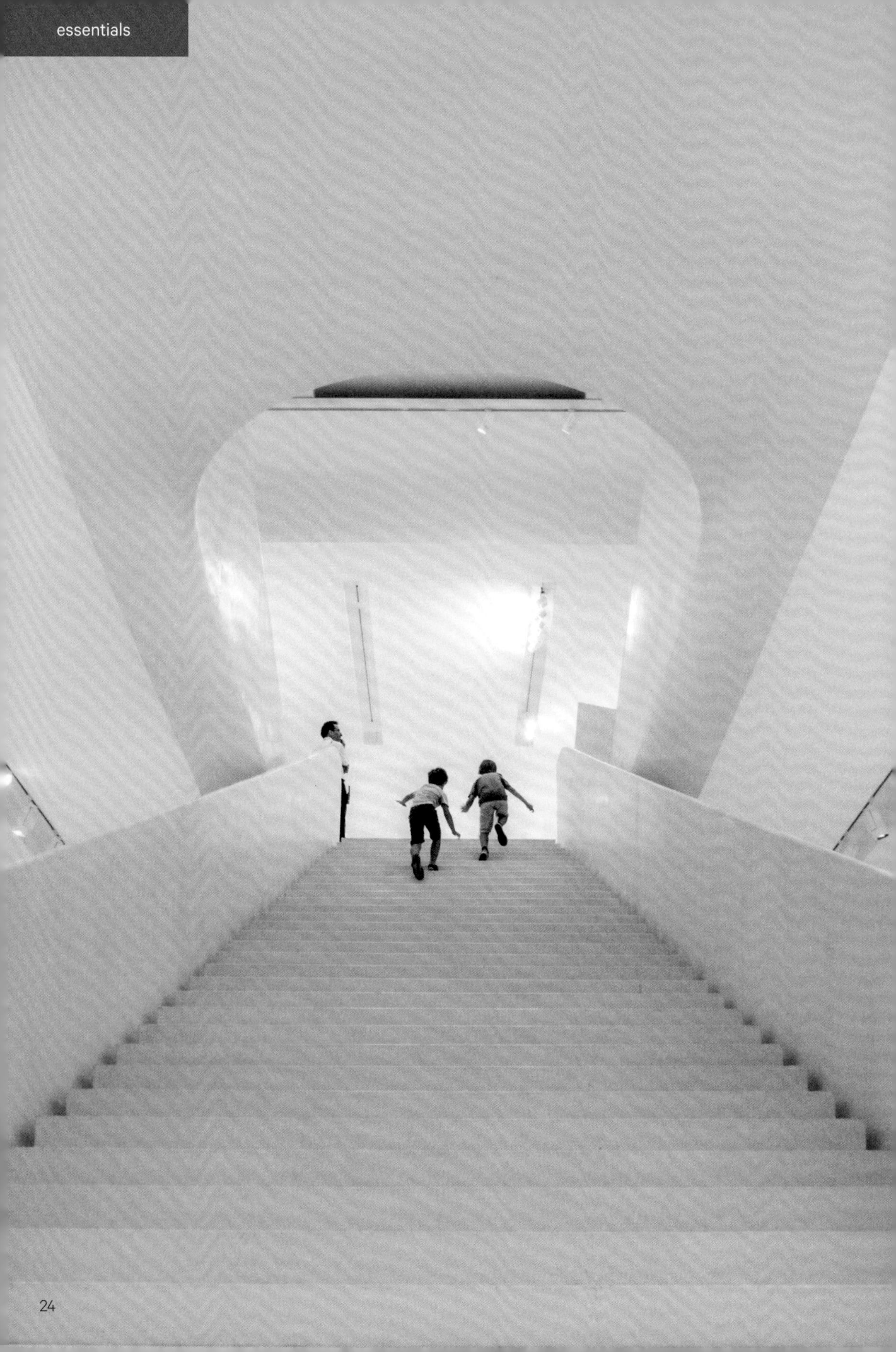

Visas and Work Permits

EU, EEA (European Economic Area) citizens and Swiss nationals do not require entry visas and are free to live and work in Germany indefinitely, but non-EU citizens must obtain the necessary work and residence permits. Generally, all foreigners planning a stay of more than three months or planning to work in Germany require visas, and, depending on your citizenship, you may have to apply in advance. For a work permit, you'll need a contract or letter of intent from your employer. If self-employed, you'll need a business plan showing your income and means to support yourself. Once the work agency (arbeits agentur) in Germany has approved your work permit, you can apply for a residence permit from the Auslanderbehorde (foreigners registration offices) in Germany or at your local German consulate or embassy. Visit auswaertiges-amt.de/en for more information. If you're looking for foreign investment, it's important to note that, in most cases, an investor will want to see your valid residence and work permits, and since this can take three months or longer, ensure you start the process early.

See **Important Government Offices** page **237**

Taxes

Navigating a new tax system as a business owner and employer can be daunting because of the complexities. Tax in Germany is no different, and it pays to use a tax advisor (*Steuerberater*), especially in the beginning. There are two main taxes on earnings, and they only differ in the way they are collected. *Lohnsteuer* (wage tax) is collected at source and paid to the tax office (*Finanzamt*), while *Einkommensteuer* (income tax) is paid by the individual when tax returns are filed (by 31 May). As a startup, you'll need to understand *Gewerbesteuer*, which is tax on all turnover. In addition, sales taxes impact both individuals and businesses. Value added tax (*Mehrwertsteuer*) applies to both goods and services and is currently 19 percent. Certain products may be eligible for reduced rate tax, and there are also exemptions to be aware of. The local Finanzamt offers support in German and English.

See **Accountants** page **236**

Starting a Company

Your first port of call for information about starting a company in Frankfurt and the Rhine-Main region is **frankfurt-main.ihk.de/english**. The Chamber of Commerce and Industry (IHK) has a wealth of information (in German and English), from developing a business plan and financing a business to writing your general terms and conditions of business (*Allgemeine Geschäftsbedingungen - AGB*) and contracts. The trade office must be notified when you start a new business or trade activity in Germany. Register at the *Ordnungsamt* (regulatory authority) and show your identification and a valid visa, including permission to start a business in Germany. Knowing what to do in an unfamiliar place can be daunting, but support is available both in person and online. The IHK has a dedicated resource center located at the *Börse* (stock exchange) in the city center. You can also contact start zero (**start-zero.de/en**), a company that specializes in growing early-stage startups and helping you build your network.

See **Programs** page **234**

Opening a Bank Account

An EC card (Euro-cheque card/*Girocard*) is the most widely-accepted bank card in Germany. However, many cafes, bars and restaurants still only accept cash, so you'll need to carry money with you. A bank account enables you to rent an apartment more easily, set up utilities and get a mobile phone contract. To open an account, you must show your ID/passport, registration document (*Meldebescheinigung*) and a valid visa (for non-EU citizens). The most common banks with physical branches are Commerzbank, Deutsche Bank, Sparkasse and Postbank. Some may charge a monthly fee for a standard checking account (*Girokonto*), and you may be charged to make withdrawals from ATMs not supported by your bank. Popular online-only options include ING DiBa or N26, and may offer services such as free cash withdrawals, English banking apps and Visa/Mastercard credit cards. All of these banks have business bank account options. Before applying, check whether they offer face-to-face support (if needed) and services in English.

See **Banks** page **236**

Getting Around

The Rhine-Main region is well-connected by public transport (provided by *RMV Rhein-Main-Verkehrsverbund*, **rmv.de**), including underground, overground and intercity trains, trams and buses. Frankfurt International Airport is fifteen minutes away from Frankfurt main station (*Hauptbahnhof*). Weekly, monthly and yearly tickets bring down the cost of travel compared to daily tickets, and if you're travelling around Germany or Europe regularly by train, it's worth buying a BahnCard.

It's not essential to own a car in Frankfurt. There are car-sharing schemes, such as Car2Go and cityFlitzer, offering pay-as-you-go options. Finding on-street car parking can be difficult and renting a space expensive. If you need to travel by car, look out for park-and-ride places across Hessen, which avoids driving into the city centers even if you live a little further afield (**pundr.de**). If you prefer to get around under your own steam, walking and cycling are equally pleasant and safe. Bike rental is possible, with extensive pick-up and drop-off locations.

Phone and Internet

In comparison to other countries, mobile phone and internet plans are on the expensive side. Contracts are normally a minimum of two years, and you should watch out for automatic renewals. If you cancel early, you'll still pay the remaining balance. On a positive note, EU roaming charges are a thing of the past, so you can use your mobile call and data allowance in any EU country. The best coverage tends to be from T-Mobile, Vodafone and O2. You can get home and business internet through these providers, but also check out Unitymedia, 1&1 Internet and Congstar. Unlimited data plans are relatively new and come at a high price (around €80 on Vodafone). Expect to pay around €20 for 10GB.

Some choose prepaid plans for more flexibility. For both prepaid and long-term contracts, you'll need to show proof of ID and a valid German address. Contracts are normally in German, and customer support in English varies.

Learning the Language

While Frankfurt is a very international city and you'll hear English being spoken everywhere, learning German will make life easier. You'll feel at home more quickly if you know how to order in a restaurant or pick up fresh bread from the bakery. The German people also really appreciate the effort. A lot of documentation for setting up a business, including contracts and insurance, is in German. Seek someone who can help translate before signing on the dotted line. Outside the cities, English is spoken at varying levels and in some cases not at all.

Apps like Duolingo are great for learning the basics, and there are hundreds of free videos on YouTube. There are numerous language schools in Frankfurt, from the Volkshochschule to Goethe Institute, or you may prefer private tuition. With Austria, Switzerland and Belgium as neighbors, knowing a little bit of German will take you a long way.

See **Language Schools** page **237**

Meeting People

You have to play the long game when it comes to making friends as an expat or when you're new to a city. It's true, German social circles can be hard to break into, but don't let that put you off. Frankfurt is one of the most international cities in Germany, so you'll meet people from all around the world. There's an abundance of bars and clubs as well as social and sport activities. The sport clubs are a reasonable price to join, and you can do everything from basketball to rowing. **Meetup.com** is a great place to start searching what's going on, and paid membership groups like Internations can connect you with other like-minded people. Facebook is bursting with meetup groups and exciting events taking place across the region. Networking events are a great way to connect with other startup founders and entrepreneurs, and the city's coworking spaces run many evening meetups. Everyone's very friendly and you can quickly build your support network.

See **Startup Events** page **238**

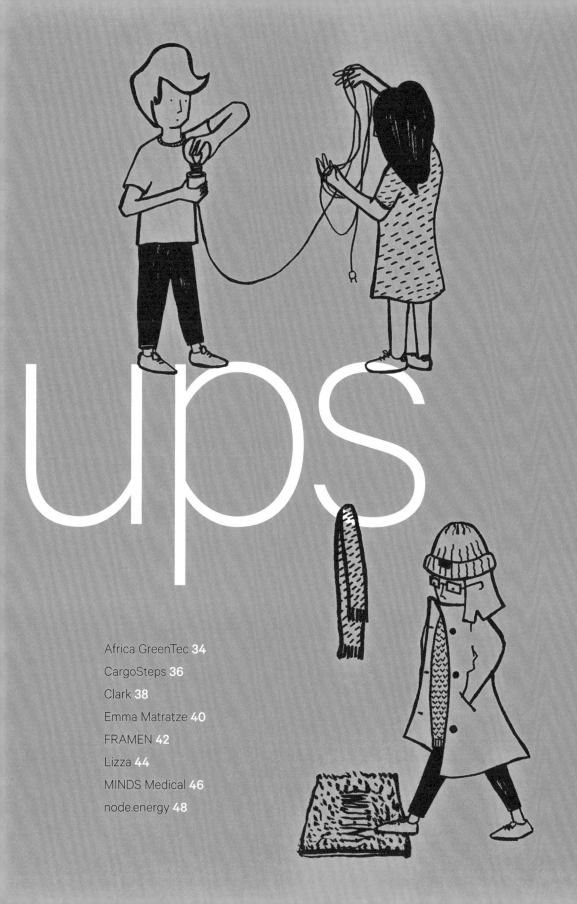

ups

[Name]
Africa GreenTec

[Elevator Pitch]
"We aim to become one of the largest eco-driven, renewable decentralized energy, water and communications providers in the Global South by empowering people toward self-determination and prosperity."

[The Story]
Africa GreenTec is the startup behind the Solartainer, a mobile 50 kW power plant that provides power, water and internet to rural areas in Africa. Founder and CEO Torsten Schreiber started the company in 2014 after the Minister of Energy of Mali invited him to exchange knowledge on energy contracting and efficiency. Torsten visited one of Mali's 1950s diesel power plants, which had barely over 13 percent energy efficiency. "It was a shock and revelation, and the most important moment in my professional life to date," he says. "As a climate change activist, I knew I could change things."

Torsten sought investors to finance a waste-incineration plant for Bamako but received no investment opportunities as there were fears of a coup in landlocked Mali. He suggested moving the vital parts of the plant to Senegal himself, as a precaution. "The potential investors were intrigued and surprised, realizing this would indeed be a mobile asset with a much higher collateral valuation." He then innovated a prototype for investor-based crowdfunding, financing the Solartainer directly through German investors and paving the way for others to finance this way. "We sell electricity and water, and with the payments from our customers, we pay back the financing," he says. The company's approach is to value the local population and "empower them with independence and objectives, which builds self-esteem and prosperity."

[Funding History]

External

In 2012, Torsten set up the Federal Association for Crowdfunding, making crowd-investing prototypes possible. The Solartainer startup team collected over €100,000 in 2015 via crowdfunding, and one year later they raised €1 million via other crowdfunding campaigns and equity rounds. To finance fifty Solartainers, they created a €10 million German bond for professional social impact investors.

[Milestones]
- Creating our Solartainer "Amali" prototype, which allows us to build three per month.
- Visiting ten countries and working closely with six presidents in Africa.
- Creating a crowd-investing innovation, allowing investors in Europe to directly finance projects in Africa.
- Becoming the first entrepreneur to secure a German-government guarantee on his investment in Africa.

[Links]   Web: africagreentec.com Facebook: AfricaGreenTec Twitter: @africagreentec

[Name]
CargoSteps

[Elevator Pitch]
"We're a B2B logistics platform for automating backloads, the extra packages a courier picks up on their return journey, built on a cross-company solution for tracking and tracing packages."

[The Story]
CargoSteps was founded on the insight that communication in the logistics industry doesn't have to be as painful and broken as it currently is. The logistics and transport companies who must work together to transport express and courier goods currently communicate over phone, email, text message and WhatsApp. "We knew what we needed, but couldn't find it. So we decided to build it ourselves," says Murat Karakaya, COO at CargoSteps. The team created a web and mobile app for couriers, with an API to integrate into existing logistics tracking systems. The platform tracks backloads (packages that can be transported by a courier on their way back to home base), allowing courier drivers to earn extra money and CargoSteps to receive a commission. The algorithm also proactively checks the status of shipments and automatically updates all stakeholders, saving time and money.

All of the cofounders have experience in the logistics and transportation industry. Rachid Touzani, the CEO, previously ran his own company, which is also where he met Murat, who worked there for four years. The cofounders started working on CargoSteps in August of 2015 and officially founded the company in 2016. They now have two offices in Frankfurt: one in the city center and the other at the Frankfurt airport House of Logistics & Mobility.

[Funding History]

Bootstrap

Seed

The CargoSteps founders were putting their own money into the business and working for free in August, 2015. In September 2016, they received €200,000 equity funding, the only external financing to date. They have also won grants from the European Space Agency, the Frankfurt founders prize, and an office at Frankfurt airport.

[Milestones]
- Crossing the one thousand customer mark in 2018.
- Launching the CargoSteps Track and Trace solution in summer 2016.
- Receiving equity funding in Sept 2016.
- Getting the first integrations into other freight forwarding systems, giving us two thousand to three thousand more customers in one sweep.

[Links]   Web: **cargosteps.de** Facebook: **CargoSteps**

[Name]

Clark

[Elevator Pitch]

"We combine cutting-edge technology with personal service and make the complex world of insurance easy, understandable and transparent."

[The Story]

Clark, a robo-advisor for insurance, was founded in 2015 by Dr. Christopher Oster, Steffen Glomb, Dr. Marco Adelt and Chris Lodde. Based in Frankfurt and Berlin, Clark has made a rapid transition from their beginnings into being a digital insurance broker market leader in Germany. "Christopher basically started Clark as a personal insurance broker for family and friends." says Marco. Subsequently, they ended up building an autonomous advisory system for insurance that they knew they could roll out and scale big. "Over the last two years, we've increased our customer base to one hundred and fifty thousand customers," he says.

The Clark iOS, Android and web apps allow the managing of a wide range of insurance services such as legal, household, health, accident and car insurances. The Clark team has developed algorithms that analyze the customers' current insurance coverage and automatically search for and recommend new and better coverage solutions at the most favorable price. The company makes its revenue from management and administration fees paid by insurance companies and with commission on any new policy taken out.

[Funding History]

Seed   External

Clark closed their first seed round of €2 million in 2015 followed by a Series A of €13 million from yabeo capital, Kulczyk Investments, HitFox and TA Ventures in 2016. In early 2018, they closed a Series B round of €25 million led by Portag3 Ventures and White Star Capital.

[Milestones]

- Closing a successful Series A round in 2015.
- Launching our website and going live in 2016.
- Getting our first TV spot in SevenVentures (ProSieben) network.
- Launching our first white label customer in 2017.

[Links]   Web: **clark.de** Facebook: **ClarkGermany** Twitter: **@ClarkGermany**

[Name]
Emma Matratze

[Elevator Pitch]

"We are setting out to revolutionize how people buy their mattresses while also providing a great night's sleep. We have received several awards and are one of the top three bed-in-a-box brands in Europe."

[The Story]

The team at Emma Matratze, founded as a subsidiary of the Bettzeit group in 2015, understands the pain of having to buy a new mattress, such as visiting many stores to try out mattresses, only to forget what the last mattress felt like. Emma Matratze offers a one-hundred-night trial and a ten-year warranty on their mattresses. Customers order a mattress online, and it's delivered in a box to their home in a matter of days. "We are convenience driven," says Max Laarmann, founder and managing director. Max has a background in food-delivery startups in Asia, and his cofounders from the Bettzeit Group have experience in mattress development. Their main focus is on creating a great product for customers by turning customer feedback into product development. "We develop the mattress close to our customers' feedback, and that's how we improve our products," says Max.

Emma Matratze started with only one type of mattress and now offers three different styles, along with other bed equipment. The team, which counts nearly two hundred people from over thirty countries, is entirely based in Frankfurt. They aim to continue creating agile business processes internally and to maintain sustainable growth. After two and a half years, Emma Matratze sells mattresses in sixteen countries and has sold more than 250,000 mattresses online.

[Funding History]

Angel

External

Emma Matratze is a 100 percent subsidiary of the Bettzeit Group and more than two thirds of the shares are with the cofounders. The Bettzeit Group provides financial support as well as know-how and a highly skilled team to support Emma Matratze. They raised funding for product optimization, establishing their own mattress laboratory and international expansion.

[Milestones]

- Hitting the 250,000 mattresses sold milestone in 2018
- Being ranked the fastest-growing startup in Europe for 2018 by Tech5
- Receiving lots of product awards across Europe, including being at the top of the Which? mattress ranking in June 2018
- Adopting an agile strategy by working in squad teams.

[Links]

Web: **emma-matratze.de** Facebook: **Emma.matratze.de** Twitter: **@emma_matratze**

[Name]
FRAMEN

[Elevator Pitch]
"We revolutionize the way people experience photography and consume it in everyday life by allowing you to stream high-quality photos to any screen. We stream photo playlists to any internet-enabled device, including tablets, TVs and more."

[The Story]
When Dimitri Gärtner, founder and CEO of FRAMEN, became a father in 2016, he realized there were many high-quality photos on his phone that he'd never see again. Plus, when he shared photos, the quality was reduced by social media websites, and many photo-display devices on the market used old technology. For Dimitri, it seemed obvious to use the high-quality devices, smart TVs, tablets and even mobile phones that are already in our homes to display photos when they're in standby mode. "Most screens are black screens," Dimitri says. "Why not turn them into photo-streaming devices?"

With some early validation from family and friends, Dimitri put together a prototype with the Raspberry Pi and began selling it to friends. He created FRAMEN to easily stream photos to connected devices over wifi, turning previously dark spaces into beautiful, inspiring photo displays. The startup gained further market validation after winning the WeWork Creator Awards and successfully completing a crowdfunding campaign to boost the production of devices. Active only since April 2018, FRAMEN has surpassed 100,000 curated photo playlists and millions of app store impressions worldwide and is generating revenue from the sales of smart devices and premium subscriptions. It has started to sell to consumers with a freemium model and, with its enterprise, it's also entering TV screens in restaurants, hotels, offices and more.

[Funding History]

Bootstrap   Pre-Seed

The initial financing came from Dimitri's own pocket and from the first sales of devices. In 2017, FRAMEN won the WeWork Creator Awards, and in July 2018 it successfully crowdfunded $100,000. This round of financing is supporting their first developer hires.

[Milestones]
- Receiving over $100,000 crowdfunding through Kickstarter in July 2018.
- Releasing four apps in April 2018.
- Winning the WeWork Creator Award.
- Working with engineers at Zühlke for three months to create the FRAMEN Player MVP.

[Links]   Web: **myframen.com** Facebook: **myframen** Twitter: **@myframen**

[Name]

Lizza

[Elevator Pitch]

"We make the world's healthiest pizza. It has barely any carbohydrates, a lot of protein, a lot of fiber, and omega-3 fatty acids, and it's made of organic flaxseed and chia seeds."

[The Story]

Lizza is a health-food startup specializing in flaxseed pizza crusts, wraps and a growing number of culinary innovations. Founded in 2015, the company boasts of having the healthiest pizza crust in the world. Cofounder Matthias Kramer created the startup by happy accident when he and cofounder Marc Schlegel cooked the recipe for a startup-brainstorming event with close friends. Their friends were impressed with the flaxseed pizza recipe and encouraged them to market the product. At the time, there were no low-carb or flaxseed pizza crusts in Germany. "We would be hardcore customers of this product," says Matthias.

In 2015, Lizza opened as a food truck. After a year interacting with customers and improving the recipe, they sold the truck and invested in a small production facility to focus solely on selling the crust. Lizza gained attention via Facebook ads and went from ten thousand orders during six months to twenty-two thousand orders a week after being featured on the show *Die Höhle der Löwen*, a German *Shark Tank*-style program. In 2017, the company branched out into other products, such as wraps, and it now sells principally online, with five thousand retailers also stocking their products. "What we sell is healthy convenience," says Matthias. "People now realize how important diet is and are spending more money on good food. That's why we succeed."

[Funding History]

Bootstrap   Angel   External

Initially, Lizza received a loan from a friend and did some self-financing. In 2016, the company received angel investment and then VC funds from *Die Höhle der Löwen*. They have since held two more internal shareholder investment rounds and closed a crowdfunding round of €1.7 million. Lizza has also received cashflow from product sales.

[Milestones]

- Listening to the market by accident and creating a startup on the reaction of close friends.
- Creating a single shippable product after conducting accidental market research interacting with six thousand to seven thousand customers.
- Going digital with a product that is normally not sold digitally.
- Consolidating a large catalogue of products to a single sellable product.

[Links]

Web: lizza.de Facebook: leckerlizza Twitter: @leckerlizza

[Name]
MINDS Medical

[Elevator Pitch]
"We automate medical coding with artificial intelligence. Hospitals can automate their reimbursement process, and health and life insurance companies can automate their underwriting."

[The Story]
Lukas Naab, cofounder of MINDS Medical, first realized in 2009 there was a big problem to solve for doctors when a doctor-friend explained how much time she spent inputting medical code (the alphanumeric system used to describe all diseases and maladies in medical records). Through further research, he found that Germany's medical coding industry is worth $1 billion in labor costs. "It's absurd that young doctors spend time doing this rather than spending time with patients," says Lukas. His friend of twenty years, Matthias Bay, built a software prototype for MINDS Medical in 2015, and they were joined by a third founder. In 2016 all three quit their full-time jobs to join the University of Frankfurt startup incubator.

The team started selling subscriptions to hospitals, but it was slow; their sales cycle was twelve to twenty-four months. A few months before their funding ran dry, a big clinical group stopped a deal at a late stage, and the third founder left. But Matthias and Lukas decided to continue building MINDS Medical until the money ran out. When they met the CEO of DFV, a private insurance company in Frankfurt, they realized their business model also worked for insurance companies, a $10 billion market. After that, things began to move quickly. They survived 2017, raised angel investment in early 2018, and are now a team of eight people.

[Funding History]

Pre-Seed

Angel

MINDS Medical received a €125,000 grant from EXIST in 2016. They also received a low-six-digit-number funding round from five business angels in the Frankfurt area in February 2018. In May, 2018 they won the Frankfurt founder's prize, and they hope to receive another round of funding by the end of 2018.

[Milestones]
- Receiving the EXIST funding grant of €125,000.
- Going full time. This was an "oh shit, we will really do this" moment.
- Showing the working prototype to our customers. In Germany, we are tech-skeptical.
- Losing the first big deal and a cofounder two months before our money ran out.
- Integration of our software with the backend of our first customer's system.

[Links]
Web: **minds-medical.de** Facebook: **MINDSMedical** Twitter: **@MindsNaab**

[Name] # node.energy

[Elevator Pitch] *"We provide software and services to industrial and commercial clients so they can efficiently plan and manage their own local power production. This saves them money and reduces overall CO_2 emissions."*

[The Story] node.energy was founded in 2016 by Matthias Karger and Lars Rinn and is the second clean-energy business started by Matthias. The pair met when Lars was a working student on Matthias' team at his previous company. Lars later created opti.node, the core software element of node.energy, and Matthias provided the market insights. The software is the first in the world to be able to optimize financial returns on microgrids by allocating locally-produced energy to consumers nearby. Their customers are industrial and commercial clients who wish to move to local, renewable power production but struggle with the complex legal and administrative requirements. The company operates on a SaaS business model and aims to provide a full-service power optimization and management package to their customers. "We have customers from many different segments – from industrial clients and agriculture to hospitals and housing – but sales and training efforts differ a great deal across these segments," says Matthias.

They are currently a team of nine people with a mix of software developers, engineers and energy market experts. Though node.energy already has thirty paying customers, some of whom have multiple power plants across Germany, the team is looking for the ideal product/market fit to scale up. "node.energy is our way to create a climate-friendly energy landscape," says Matthias.

[Funding History]

Bootstrap

Seed

Angel

node.energy was initially a bootstrapped startup. Matthias decided to reinvest some money from a previous company's exit into node.energy. The team raised a seed round from local angel investors that was led by High-Tech Gründerfonds and may raise a Series A in the future.

[Milestones]
- Successfully testing our business model with pilot customers.
- Raising a seed fundraising round.
- Launching the software to the market.

[Links] Web: **node.energy** Twitter: **@node_energy**

rams

- **Have a founding team.**
  Startups should have at least two founders
  who are committed to the business full time.

- **Have a working product.**
  You'll need to have at least one client who is paying
  to use your product in your home market, and you
  should be ready to scale to new markets.

- **Show us your track record.**
  We want to see what you have achieved to date – this
  means showing us your clients and market traction.

- **Have a plan for the future.**
  Those who get the most out of the accelerator
  program are those who have a plan for what they
  want to do and achieve in the next year, and maybe
  longer term.

- **Travel to Frankfurt.**
  Startups should be a registered business somewhere
  in the world, and founders should be ready to travel
  to Frankfurt for three or four days out of each month
  of the program.

[Name]
Accelerator Frankfurt

[Elevator Pitch]
"We're the gateway to the financial market in Germany for startups. We help advanced-stage startups who have paying customers and products get into the German market through our three-month, sales-focused acceleration program."

[Sector]
Fintech, B2B

[Description]
Accelerator Frankfurt was founded in 2016 by Ram Shoham and Maria Pennanen, based on their first-hand experience of seeing the corporates where they worked not being able to partner with startups. "We wanted to set up this program as an interface for corporates and startups," says Ram. Because of Ram and Maria's professional backgrounds and Frankfurt's draw as a financial hub, they focus on fintech, but they also work with startups in cybersecurity, blockchain, proptech and more. Since 2016, they have accelerated thirty startups through the program, which runs twice a year in Frankfurt.

The Accelerator Frankfurt program helps startups enter the German market by providing introductions to banks. During the three-month program, startups also have a dedicated lead mentor, free office space, client meetings and workshops focused on commercial viability, legal, regulation, digital marketing and investment. The program is equity free, but startups pay a participation fee and success fee on revenue generated from clients introduced by Accelerator Frankfurt. What differentiates this program from other accelerators is that they work with many banks as partners, whereas other programs tend to work with just one partner. The secret to their successful collaborations is a deep understanding of the needs of their forty banking partners. "We find what the banks are looking for, bring these innovations into the program, and connect the two," says Ram.

Many startups who join the accelerator are referred by someone in the network, be it an investor, mentor or alumni. Interested startups can apply via the Accelerator Frankfurt website. Maria and Ram advise young startups to have a deep understanding of the market and the problem their company solves, and a fantastic team who can execute no matter what. "One of the important qualities in founders is endurance, because startup life is hard and stressful," says Maria. "You need to have the right mindset, take risks and work hard."

[Apply to]
acceleratorfrankfurt.com/startups

[Links]
Web: acceleratorfrankfurt.com Facebook: acceleratorfrankfurt Twitter: @accelerator_ffm

- **Be authentic.**
  We want to work with founders who are comfortable
  in their own skin and are not afraid to be themselves.

- **Bring knowledge of your market niche.**
  If you don't have people with expertise in marketing
  or finance, that's okay. If you don't have anyone on
  your team who really knows your market, that's
  not good.

- **Be in it for the long run.**
  We want founders who aren't looking for a short-term
  exit but are in it to build a sustainable company.

- **Be in Frankfurt.**
  The programs take place in the Frankfurt region,
  and we want all participants to be on-site in order
  to get the most value from the program.

- **Speak German.**
  Most of the program content takes place in German,
  so a good working knowledge of the language
  will help.

- **Know your whys.**
  You should know why your business exists and what
  impact you want to create.

[Name]
black chili

[Elevator Pitch]
"We're the first company builder in Frankfurt with a passion to support and develop impact businesses. In our black chili academy, we deliver a three-step collaborative and customized business-building system in our own coworking space."

[Sector]
Sustainability

[Description]
black chili was founded in 2014 as a service provider for freelancers. In 2016, they moved from helping small agencies to helping startups by founding a company builder and academy. This is in addition to their corporate innovation consulting services, which bring the startup and corporate mindsets together. Their focus is on building sustainable businesses with the potential to grow. To join the black chili company builder, founders should be committed to their ideas for the long run. "Our idea was that from day one, you can learn how to be an entrepreneur, have your own startup, and really take responsibility as a founder," says Recai Gündüz, CEO and founder of black chili.

Startups that join the company builder are generally at the idea stage, but can also be at a later stage. A dedicated coach is assigned to the founders by the black chili team, and this coach creates a tailored support plan to develop the company. The program also provides workshops and skilled mentors in marketing, sales, finance and administration, and if the startup is growing fast, black chili will assist with recruiting, HR and leadership coaching. Every three to six months, teams have a progress check-in with the black chili team. Their network of investors, other startup founders in the Rhine Main region and contacts at the top one hundred corporates in Germany is opened up to the founders. The black chili company builder has created five companies and is "just getting started," according to Recai.

To get involved, startups can join CoWorkPlay (the coworking space associated with black chili), take part in their startup academy, or apply to join the company builder by sending the team a pitch deck and cover letter online via the black chili website. The cover letter should explain what makes the startup special, why it's an impact company and what impact it will have. Recai's advice to founders is to be themselves during the application process.

[Apply to]
academy@blackchili.de

[Links]
Web: **blackchili.de** Facebook: **blackchiliGmbH** Twitter: **@blackchili**

- **Have a link to a university in Frankfurt Rhine-Main.**
  One of the team members should be a student,
  alumni, faculty or staff of Goethe University or
  another university in Frankfurt Rhine-Main area.

- **Have a diverse team.**
  It's very important that the team members have
  different educational backgrounds and experiences.

- **Bring a scalable, new and innovative idea.**
  There should be a certain prospect of growth
  connected to the market and to the business model.

- **Have a business model.**
  The market potential has to be big, and the team
  should be thinking about how the business model
  will work.

- **Be present in Frankfurt.**
  We've learned from experience that the teams who
  work in the office space in Frankfurt usually have
  faster success.

Goethe Unibator

[Name]

[Elevator Pitch]

"We are a bridge between research and commercialization at Goethe University. We are fostering entrepreneurial thinking and action by supporting promising early-stage entrepreneurial ventures from Goethe University."

[Sector]

Fintech, medtech, other

[Description]

Acting as the gateway from research to business, the Goethe Unibator wants to invest in people who are turning cutting-edge research into scalable businesses. "One of the most important things is the team," says Katharina Funke-Braun, managing director of Goethe Unibator. "And of course, the idea has to be innovative and scalable, otherwise we wouldn't talk about startups."

The stage of startups accepted to the program varies from idea stage, with no company registration, to companies that have already raised funding. There is a focus on fintech, as the Goethe Unibator belongs to the Department of Economics, but the portfolio ranges from the food industry to PR, lifestyle and medtech. To apply, startups must fill in an online application and submit an idea paper, and then present their idea at selection day in front of the Unibator team and selected mentors. The selection day doubles as the biggest networking event for the Goethe Unibator, where mentors and alumni are invited to join.

Accepted startups spend their time at the Goethe Unibator office space at the university in Frankfurt. The program consists of eighteen months of incubation, or bootcamp, where startups can participate in workshops and access a network of mentors from across business functions, including marketing, finance, venture capital and legal specialists. Support from mentors is primarily on-demand and driven by the startups. "Anytime they need support, I tell them who they should ask for help," says Katharina. Goethe Unibator also offers support to startups for applications to different funding options in Germany, including the EXIST Gründerstipendium, a scholarship for entrepreneurs just out of university in Germany. After the bootcamp, startups present the progress they have made at an Evaluation Day to the management team. Startups who are fundraising and can show growth and paying customers can present at the Pitch Club to external investors.

[Apply to]

goetheunibator.de/apply1-2

[Links]

Web: **goetheunibator.de** Facebook: **goetheunibator** Twitter: **@GUnibator**

- **Already have seed funding.**
  You should have financial resources that will last
  for the time that you're in the program; i.e., by way
  of having been previously funded.

- **Have market traction.**
  We want to see that you've acquired some first users,
  partnerships, paying customers or media awareness.

- **Have a completed high-tech prototype.**
  You should have a usable product that's sales-ready
  or at least in the PoC stage.

- **Have an exceptional team.**
  Your company should have a complementary and
  experienced founders team – no first-time founders.

[Name] # GTEC

[Elevator Pitch] *"We're the first private-sector, open ecosystem for entrepreneurship in Europe. Our vision is to unlock the potential of entrepreneurship and technology to enable a desirable and sustainable future."*

[Sector] **Corporate innovation, community, startup programs**

[Description] *Forbes* has referred to GTEC (German Tech Entrepreneurship Center) as Germany's one-stop collaboration shop for European startups. GTEC's mission is to inspire people, guide entrepreneurs and grow sustainable companies. It has a number of initiatives designed to address challenges through the application of technology, assisting corporates in mastering the digital world and providing academia with the tools and knowledge to educate the next generation of changemakers and entrepreneurs.

GTEC takes no equity and has two primary offerings for startups: Soft-Landing and the No Bullshit Lab. Soft-Landing, a project funded by the European Union under the Horizon 2020 initiative, provides scaling support to European, American and Indian startups. The intensive one-week program takes place in different locations around the world, including Paris, Berlin, Zoetermeer, Vilnius and Silicon Valley. Startups get help in discovering new markets and learning how to scale abroad, and there's the possibility of extending the trip to a month. The No Bullshit Lab doesn't concern itself with regimented structures of workshops, lectures or any predefined curriculum. The focus is solely on supporting startups and helping them to develop and expand by giving them access to experienced entrepreneurs, mentors, corporate partners and alumni.

GTEC also runs education programs that teach the entrepreneur mindset to top-level executives and students at leading educational institutions. It engages with thought leaders in training courses, workshops and keynotes, and works with some of the world's leading entrepreneurs. For national and international universities, GTEC provides the tools to study and teach entrepreneurship and helps to integrate up-to-date expertise into existing academic programs through leading entrepreneurs. It has central coworking spaces in Frankfurt and Berlin, and access can be granted from between three to twelve months. The GTEC team is always on hand to answer any questions, and if they can't help, one of GTEC's extensive network of fellow startups, investors and mentors most certainly can.

[Apply to] **gtec.center/startups**

[Links] Web: **gtec.center** Facebook: **GTECcenter** Twitter: **@GTECcenter** Instagram: **gteccenter**

- **Have a great team.**
  Your team should have worked together successfully in the past and be open to coaching. You should be able to explain why your team is best suited to build and scale this business.

- **Have deep insight into your market.**
  You should offer experience, connections and a deep understanding of the sector you're seeking to disrupt.

- **Have great products that will disrupt large and/or growing markets.**
  Are you targeting a large and/or growing market? Have you achieved product-market fit, or are you likely to find it soon? Why will your product win the market over?

- **Show you have traction.**
  How many clients or users are actively using your product? Are they paying for it? How quickly are you growing?

Merck Accelerator

[Name]

[Elevator Pitch] *"We are looking for real partners so that we can work together in shaping the future. With programs in our headquarters in Germany, in China and our Satellites events in Africa, startups can find their perfect fit and connect to our global network for collaboration."*

[Sector] Healthcare, life sciences, performance materials, bio-sensing and interfaces, clean meat, liquid biopsy.

[Description] The Merck Accelerator, running since 2015, helps entrepreneurs to connect with and build up corporate partnerships with the Merck Group, who are multinational specialists in healthcare, life sciences, and performance materials. Startups get the chance to know Merck and learn the needs and activities of an established corporate, while the company explores interesting approaches beyond pitch decks and conference calls with the startups involved. Munya Chivasa, the head of Merck Accelerator, says, "Our corporate accelerator is focused on exploring new technologies and trends from different startup ecosystems."

The Merck Accelerator, housed in the corporate headquarters Innovation Center, identifies opportunities for partnerships with startups, creates an environment in which startups exchange their innovations with internal Merck employees and connect to trending ecosystems in China and the Silicon Valley. "The main benefit for startups and for Merck is the opportunity to work side by side for three months in order to explore business opportunities and shape a pilot project," says Munya. Merck is interested in new, cutting-edge technology, and this often comes with an element of risk. This is why, according to Munya, "we constantly advise teams to find good partners who are in it for the long-term and who support in reducing costs and hurdles." The accelerator wants Merck to be that partner for accepted startups.

Startups accepted into the Merck Accelerator get access to Merck's brand new infrastructure, including a modern office and a Makerspace for rapid prototyping. There is also a hands-on curriculum where participants learn from successful founders and interact with internal innovation project teams. Merck's curriculum covers topics ranging from HR management to IP law and regulatory issues. Startups enrolled in the Merck Accelerator can meet external investors, explore opportunities in Merck's China Innovation Hub, and apply for up to €50,000 in funding. This exemplifies the main upside to Merck's Accelerator program, which is constant contact with corporate innovators, access to cutting-edge technology, and the chance to learn by corporate example.

[Apply to] accelerator@merckgroup.com

[Links] Web: accelerator.merckgroup.com Facebook: merckgroup Twitter: @merckgroup

- Have a team of more than one person with
  complementary skill sets.
  We believe that, most of the time, solving problems
  comes from conversations with people from diverse
  backgrounds.

- Identify the problem from the consumer's
  perspective.
  You should also be able to provide a solution that
  is ten times better than anything that is already
  available on the market.

- Prove your technical and executional skill set.
  Your team should be able to prove you can make
  the business model work with early revenue
  and a working product.

- Be fully committed to the project.
  Founders should not only be committed to executing
  tasks at the company but also be committed to the
  vision of the company.

[Name]
PANDO. Ventures

[Elevator Pitch]
"We're an early-stage startup-accelerator program that creates individualized programs tailored to you. Founding teams receive hands-on support from experienced entrepreneurs and access to a broad network of partners, business angels, corporate partners and VCs."

[Sector]
Technology, B2C and B2B

[Description]
In 2016, a group of cofounders in the Frankfurt region decided to start a people-focused accelerator program (PANDO. Ventures) and a digital consultancy (PANDO. Services). "PANDO. Ventures is based on our own experience of starting up, getting investors on board, and inspiring people," says cofounder Chris Reimann. The team initially started working with physical products, but now focuses on accelerating a number of different digital tech business models including SaaS, online platforms, marketplaces, e-commerce and others. Early-stage startups with an idea and dedicated team are encouraged to apply to join the program via the PANDO. Ventures website. They were recently named as one of the best accelerator programs in Europe by AlphaGamma.

PANDO. Ventures is free of all limiting factors (such as time and place) for startups that wish to participate. This means there are no batches of startups and no fixed location or time-frame for startups to participate in the program. The program is tailored to the individual needs of the startups who join, and the team helps startups by providing individualized access to know-how, exclusive partners and financial capital. They also help startups by setting up their boards. "We go into the startup and work hands-on by cofounding the company, by providing operational partners and by providing know-how," says Chris. "We give our time to the startup instead of just giving money and showing them part-time where to go." In the beginning, startups meet with the PANDO. Ventures team every day, and over the course of time this decreases to monthly and quarterly board meetings. PANDO. Ventures has a large network of advisors and mentors who dedicate their time to the startups, and all its advisors and mentors have started businesses. The team plans to work with four to six startups per year.

[Apply to]
pando-ventures.com/en/apply

[Links]
Web: **pando-ventures.com** Facebook: **pando.ventures** Twitter: **@pando_ventures**

- Have a 360-degree view on things.
  You should do the necessary research in order to
  have a stable business model with a strong focus
  on empathy from your target customer group.

- Think about the sustainable development
  of your company.
  If you have to change your business plan, maintain
  your commitment to purpose to keep your targets
  consistent.

- Learn to collaborate.
  You should not only learn to utilize the resources
  of your team but collaborate, in the broader sense,
  with communities and experts outside your startup.

- Have a team with a relevant mix of skills.
  It is essential to have a diverse and well-integrated
  team and to use new methodologies such as science-
  fiction thinking and purpose thinking to envision bold
  solutions linked to the SDGs.

[Name]

SAP Next-Gen

[Elevator Pitch]

"SAP Next-Gen is a purpose-driven innovation university and community for the SAP ecosystem, enabling startups to connect with corporates, partners and universities and innovate with purpose linked to the UN Sustainable Development Goals."

[Sector]

Enterprise software applications, business networks, platforms

[Description]

SAP Next-Gen is an open community platform that drives "innovation with purpose" to support SAP's commitment to the UN's seventeen Sustainable Development Goals. The SAP Next-Gen program includes innovation tours, meetups, boot camps, startup matchmaking, advising, industry summits and a variety of projects with academia. It extends to more than 3,700 educational institutions across more than 117 countries, with a large array of startups, accelerators, VCs, futurists, SAP experts and various partners collaborating together for an innovative future. SAP Next-Gen Frankfurt enables corporates to connect with and benefit from solutions being developed by startups, and it connects startups to the broad SAP innovation ecosystem linked to SAPs global headquarters in Walldorf. Technologies that can be used in fintech, such as blockchain, are making the more legacy-oriented companies sit up and take notice, and SAP Next-Gen wants to leverage the huge potential for bringing industries together with startups.

On a global level, SAP works diligently to identify the strongest verticals of each location and make the best connections. SAP Next-Gen for enterprises connects companies with researchers, students, startups, tech community partners, experts and accelerators to brainstorm new solutions and disruptive technologies. SAP Next-Gen for youth brings relevant academic content into classrooms to help foster the next generation of developers, designers, makers and entrepreneurs. The SAP Young Thinkers program inspires school students to study STEM (science, technology, engineering and math) with a view to a future career. SAP Next-Gen Chapters around the world support educational institutions in a country or region to build up the local SAP Next-Gen innovation with purpose network. SAP Next-Gen for citizens hosts events such as meetups and festivals on topics ranging from female empowerment (#sheinnovates) to science-fiction thinking to using technology for good. SAP Next-Gen also welcomes universities across the globe to open an SAP Next-Gen Lab on campus to bring industry partners, academics, startups, tech community partners, venture firms, purpose-driven partners and SAP experts together.

[Apply to]

sapnextgen@sap.com

[Links]

Web: **sap.com/next-gen** Facebook: **SAPNextGen** Twitter: **@SAPNextGen** Instagram: **sapnextgen**

- **Be located in the Frankfurt Rhine-Main area.**
  Startup offices and innovative work settings are
  always a highlight for visitors. An office kitchen table
  or rooftop terrace make the best intimate settings
  for new ideas to flourish.

- **Have an interesting founder story.**
  People love hearing your story and learning from
  you, and your stories are invaluable additions to
  the program.

- **Have a scalable business model.**
  The program attracts many interesting participants
  who might be looking for exactly what you're offering
  and who can help you find new clients or partners.

- **Be willing to open your doors and have
  a welcoming atmosphere.**
  Organize some snacks and help promote your session
  on social media. The Startup SAFARI team will take
  care of the rest.

- **Be an early-stage startup with big ambitions.**
  The unique concept of Startup SAFARI allows you
  to gain vast visibility in the region and the global
  network. The effort is minimal and the outcome
  could be huge.

[Name]

Startup SAFARI FrankfurtRheinMain

[Elevator Pitch]

"We offer two days of open doors around the regional ecosystem, allowing the best insight into what the cities have to offer around startup and innovation."

[Sector]

Tech

[Description]

Startup SAFARI is a global movement with annual two-day events in major cities around the globe, such as in Frankfurt, Miami, Paris and Athens, with many others in the planning stages. The event, the largest decentralized startup event of its kind in the world, allows attendees to look behind the scenes of local startup ecospheres. Startups, incubators, accelerators, coworking spaces, VCs, corporate labs, universities and other key players in the ecosystem can each create an open-door event listing. Topics can be on anything that the hosts feel is relevant and informative. Potential attendees can browse the city-wide sessions and book tickets through the Startup SAFARI website.

The FrankfurtRheinMain edition offers a large array of sessions spread throughout Frankfurt, Mainz, Darmstadt, Wiesbaden and other select locations in the greater Frankfurt region. The event, which is made possible by corporate partners such as PwC, Zühlke, Hessen Trade & Invest, Deutsche Börse Group, TechQuartier, Wirtschaftsinitiative FrankfurtRheinMain and many more, attracts over five hundred participants annually. Each city has a designated event team that takes care of logistics (for example, helping participating companies to find larger event spaces for their events if needed), and for the last two years the digital consultancy Candylabs has taken the reins in Frankfurt to ensure things go smoothly.

Startup SAFARI represents an effective way to grow networks, gain visibility, find talent or partners and showcase investment opportunities. Local startups at all stages of development are warmly encouraged to take part in the event, host an event and help to represent the thriving FrankfurtRheinMain ecosystem. Startup SAFARI FrankfurtRheinMain is held every fall, and interested parties can forward online applications of interest in the preceding spring.

[Apply to]

frankfurt.startupsafari.com

[Links]   Web: frankfurt.startupsafari.com Facebook: **SAFARIFRM** Twitter: **@SAFARIFRM**

- **Be into something.**
  You should have experience behind the idea you're putting forth as well as a high level of interest and passion to keep you going in developing the idea.

- **Be open-minded.**
  Part of being a successful participant is having the ability to change your mindset as you learn and connect with others.

- **Lead dynamically.**
  Have a good understanding of your whole process so that you can delegate efficiently and successfully in a changing environment.

- **Help others accelerate.**
  If you want to win the weekend, you must be willing to share ideas, interact with other teams, and not be afraid that others will steal ideas. This is at the core of what the weekend is about, so get into the helping spirit.

[Name]
Startup Weekend Mittelhessen

[Elevator Pitch]
"We've created a weekend for people to build up their startups, share their dreams, meet each other, receive feedback from astonishing mentors and accelerate their plans to create a prospering company."

[Sector]
All tech sectors

[Description]
Established in 2016, Startup Weekend Mittelhessen is an opportunity for entrepreneurial individuals and startup teams to come together for an intensive weekend to pitch, learn and make mistakes, with the goal of turning an idea into a viable business model in just three days. "It's the experience of a bunch of crazy people with crazy ideas trying to bring their ideas forward," says Martin Lacroix, one of the main organizers and the weekend's founder. Inspired by his experience working at a business school, Martin brought the concept to Mittelhessen to help build the startup scene in a less urban region. "We offer the platform to create," he says, "and to let coincidences happen."

People come from all over the region, and the weekend is structured to fit as many activities and events as possible. A keynote address from an established startup entrepreneur opens the proceedings, followed by a rapid-fire pitch competition called the Pitch Fire and sessions in which people form new teams. Over the course of the weekend, teams who made it through the Pitch Fire hone their company pitches and receive expert mentoring, preparing to give their final pitches on Sunday. Other weekend programming includes team building, one-on-one coaching and workshops, with titles such as "Essential Growth Hacking Tactics To Get Traction and Massive Scale for Your Startup" (from the 2018 edition).

The organizers hope to foster a fun working experience and also provide resources, such as a few weeks of partner-sponsored office space for the winning team. Participants leave the weekend with broader networks and deeper connections. Mittelhessen is open to everyone, so although the majority of participants come from universities, anyone is welcome. It's especially useful for people who want a glimpse of the entrepreneurial ecosystem without having to commit to being a founder quite yet. "We always say it's much more expensive to stay away from the weekend because of what we offer," says Martin.

[Apply to]
startup-weekend-mittelhessen.de

[Links]
Web: **startup-weekend-mittelhessen.de** Facebook: **SWMittelhessen**

- **Be willing to cooperate.**
  This is a guiding principle at TechQuartier for our programs and community in general. We want people on board who are daring, curious and open to exploring with us.

- **Bring the energy with you.**
  If we can see the energy with a startup, it will make the exchange more valuable. Those are the kinds of people we like.

- **Have a scalable business.**
  We are looking for companies that already have a proven business model with a product and initial traction. The more market traction a company has, the better.

- **Be committed.**
  You should be ready to grow the business no matter what and be willing to stick it out through the good and the bad.

- **Come to Frankfurt.**
  The programs take place in person in Frankfurt, and we ask a representative from all companies to be here for a set duration of the programs.

[Name]
TechQuartier

[Elevator Pitch]
"We're an innovation hub for startups and corporates in Frankfurt. We run a number of multi-corporate accelerator programs for startups in fintech and enterprise."

[Sector]
Fintech, sportstech, agtech

[Description]
TechQuartier was established as a coworking space in Frankfurt in 2016 out of a need for a space where corporations and startups could meet and collaborate. Since then, they have become one of the main innovation hubs in Frankfurt. They provide space for coworking and events but also offer a number of acceleration programs for startups in fintech and other industries. "We strongly believe that innovation comes from making different ideas and industries collide," says Hugo Paquin, marketing manager at TechQuartier. One thing that makes TechQuartier different is that many of their accelerator programs are multi-corporate, meaning there is more than one corporation involved.

Two examples of such programs are Growth Alliance Fintech and Growth Alliance Agtech, both offering condensed programs that focus on corporate collaboration, matchmaking and getting startups valuable feedback from diverse stakeholders. These programs were designed from the lessons TechQuartier learned from running over a dozen batches of acceleration programs in just under two years. TechQuartier's partners, coming from industry, academia and their international network of mentors and investors, take part in the programs through a variety of interactive sessions. These focus on industry-specific hot topics, peer-to-peer challenges where startups receive feedback on areas of improvement, and one-on-one meetings with investors, mentors and decision makers at corporations. The programs are designed to support entrepreneurs scaling their industry-challenging ideas. "Whether you are a new or seasoned entrepreneur, TechQuartier has an added value to offer your business" says Melanie Borst, head of programs at TechQuartier.

In addition to Growth Alliance, TechQuartier runs a number of other accelerator programs in partnership with corporates, and all programs are equity free. Examples include the EY Startup Academy for early-stage startups, the MMI SportsTech accelerator program, built in collaboration with Eintracht Frankfurt, and the UX Accelerator developed with PwC, among others. Corporates interested in cocreating an innovation program or working with TechQuartier in sourcing and matching with startups can also get in touch.

[Apply to]
techquartier.com/activities/acceleration

[Links]
Web: **techquartier.com** Facebook: **TechQuartier** Twitter: **@TechQuartier**

spa

ces

[Name] # BEEHIVE

[Address]   Mainzer Landstraße 33a, 60329 Frankfurt

[Total Area]

400м²

[Workspaces]

67

[The Story]   BEEHIVE Frankfurt is one of four BEEHIVEs in Germany, with the other three located in Hamburg. They are all interlinked by the Beehive app, from which workspaces and meeting rooms can be easily booked at any time, 24/7 (subject to availability). BEEHIVE was originally set up in 2016 by real estate company alstria as a more relaxed option for those who operate outside of the regular nine to five. There is the option of three different memberships: BEE FREE (three-day trial for free), BEE OPEN (full access to all open spaces) and BEE PRIVATE (own working space).

The Frankfurt location was opened in 2017 at The Spot, a bustling building in the heart of the Fintech district of Bahnhofsviertel, which also houses Main Incubator and a number of in-house startups. BEEHIVE has an open space with a variety of private work offices, meeting facilities and recreational areas with cozy lounges, arcade games and a kitchen. "We at BEEHIVE make a point of contributing to an active community," says Katharina Waitkus, the coworking space manager, "and so we host regular events and meetups each month such as the BEE for Startup Breakfast." The space is located only five minutes away from the central train station, the S-Bahn station Taunusanlage or the subway station Willy-Brandt-Platz, and a DB-Rad station is located in front of BEEHIVE's door.

[Links]   Web: beehive.work Facebook: beehivework Twitter: @beehivework Instagram: beehive.work

Face of the Space:
Katharina Waitkus was an office-manager
trainer in Munich but decided on a change
and moved to Frankfurt in 2017 to seek
a more community-related job, which led
her to the Frankfurt startup scene.
She enjoys the unpredictable nature of
what each day will bring at BEEHIVE.

[Name]   # CoWorkPlay

[Address]   Otto-Meßmer-Straße 1, 60314 Frankfurt Eastside

[Total Area]

2,400m²

[Workspaces]

120

[The Story]   Founders Yvonne Schrodt and Jana Ehret started CoWorkPlay as a cozy place where
parents, especially women, wouldn't have to choose between family and career, and
where both parents and non-parents could work side by side. The first CoWorkPlay
location is now part of Frankfurt's biggest coworking space, Frankfurt Eastside, next
to the river and near the European Central Bank. CoWorkPlay also opened a second
inner-city location in 2018 in MyZeil. The CoWorkPlay locations have three distinct
areas – work, events and children's areas – all within easy proximity of each other.
The community manager on hand is only too happy to give advice and support
to residents, help them make useful contacts and ensure they feel welcome.

CoWorkPlay is not about a specific industry or target group but is rather intended
as a way to bring different groups and people together. "Our community is as colorful
as confetti rain," says Yvonne. "No matter if you're old or young, startup, freelancer,
parent or non-parent, we celebrate working together in a unique atmosphere.
Furthermore, we bring together what belongs together. Whether you're a lawyer,
graphic artist or table football player, as a CoWorkPlay member you benefit from
the broad supplier and startup network as well as the local experts."

[Links]   Web: co-work-play.de Facebook: coworkplay Twitter: @cowork_play Instagram: co.work.play

Face of the Space:

Yvonne Schrodt is cofounder and CEO of CoWorkPlay. Her first steps into the startup world were made during her time with company-builder black chili. She's a real organizational miracle and always stays cool, even in difficult situations. She's also married and the mother of a thirteen year-old daughter and lives at the gates of Frankfurt.

[Name] heimathafen Wiesbaden

[Address] Karlstraße 22, 65185 Wiesbaden

[Total Area]

180 M²

[Workspaces]

25

[The Story] "Of course we have to offer the right infrastructure, but what makes it really valuable is the community we bring together and the events we pull off," says Dominik Hofmann, who founded the heimathafen Wiesbaden coworking space in 2012. The space, which has been through three waves of expansion since then and now covers 180 m² across three floors, is populated by around fifteen startups and sixty freelancers.

The light, open, flex-desk workspace is equipped with a cafe and offers coworkers access to all necessary services, but its true goal is to be more than just a coworking space. The heimathafen concept is based around Dominik's "six C's": coworking, conference, cafe, community events, connect (the hub has a partner-matching platform) and consulting – for corporates looking to partner with innovators. An additional 1,800 m² space is set to open in Wiesbaden's old courthouse and will incorporate a social innovation lab and makerspace. As one of the first movers in the local coworking scene, Dominik's team had to work hard at first to explain the concept, but its reputation has now been established. "We are one of the key players, and startups and founders can sense that energy."

[Links] Web: **heimathafen-wiesbaden.de** Facebook: **heimathafenWiesbaden** Twitter: **@heimathafenwiesbaden**

Face of the Space:
Dominik Hofmann is founder and CEO
of heimathafen Wiesbaden, which he
set up alongside cofounder Abi von
Schnurbein. From a business administration
background, he was inspired to launch the
space after living for a year in New York,
where he saw what impact collaborative
hubs could have on innovation communities.

[Name] # HUB31

[Address] Hilpertstraße 31, 64295 Darmstadt

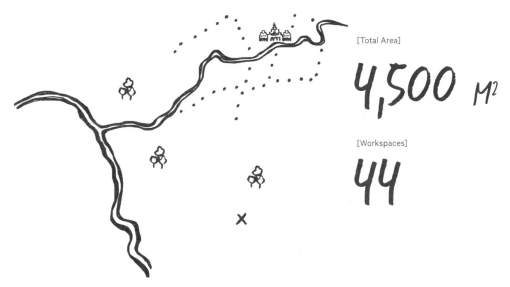

[Total Area]

4,500 M²

[Workspaces]

44

[The Story] HUB31 was built as a hub for technology startups to meet one another and get access to hardware workshops. Opened in 2018 as an addition to the Darmstadt ecosystem, the space has a dedicated and growing member base. Its focus is on actionable ways to help startups achieve their goals, and a major focus for many of its technology-based member companies is developing and testing physical products. To better support this, the space sports a shared workshop and an open laboratory for DIY entrepreneurs.

HUB31 is housed in a freshly-renovated building and sports a simple and clean aesthetic. The coworking space offers hot desks, fixed desks, private offices and modern conference rooms as well as workshops for both wood/metal processing and biology/chemistry projects. It also includes lounge areas for events, spacious areas for networking and collaboration, and even a room to sleep in for entrepreneurs planning to work through the night. HUB31 is close to major transport hubs, offers concrete support for its members with an evolving hive of hardware workshops and labs, and has as an on-site gym and plans for a large-scale food court.

[Links] Web: **hub31.de** Facebook: **HUB31Darmstadt**

Face of the Space:
Dr. Sebastian Harrach originally started out
as a strategy and technology consultant.
Before joining HUB31, he held a position
as the academic CEO of two computer
science institutes, each consisting of
about twenty researchers. Sebastian's
technological and organizational
experience and his strategic mindset
make him a perfect choice to run HUB31.

[Name] # Mindspace Eurotheum

[Address] Neue Mainzer Straße 66–68, 60311 Frankfurt

[Total Area]

3,500m²

[Workspaces]

500

[The Story] Founded in 2014 in Tel Aviv as a way to connect people and create a startup community, Mindspace is a coworking and flexible office space with twenty-five locations and more than fourteen thousand members across the globe. Members have a myriad of signup options, from open-space working to hot desks, private offices and specialized suites, as well as scale-up opportunities and a packed calendar of events. Mindspace works to make their space a home and community for their members, mixing coworking with fun activities such as networking breakfasts and personal well-being courses as well as workshops and skills training. "We have a very boutique product," says Frankfurt Senior Community Manager Florian Fellmer. "The coworkers are family."

The Frankfurt location opened in September 2018 and occupies five floors of the Eurotheum building in the heart of the city's business district. The interior has a vintage, urban-chic feel and was designed with attention to detail, down to the individual books placed within the space. All sectors and company sizes are welcome, and community managers actively connect people. The look and working environment of each Mindspace location reflects where they are situated. "We adapt to the needs of the local market," says Florian. As an added bonus, members get 24/7 access to the space. Mindspace is not only a high-end coworking space with a stunning visual aesthetic, but also a place where work teams can come together around the soda fountain or coffee bar as friends.

[Links] Web: mindspace.me/frankfurt Facebook: MindspaceFrankfurt Twitter: @MindspaceME

Face of the Space:

Florian Fellmer was born and raised close to Frankfurt and has a background in strategy consulting. He first got to know Mindspace from a member perspective. With his passion for connecting people in the startup ecosystem, he joined the coworking space as a senior community manager. The company fits his inclusive and connective entrepreneurial philosophy, and he is committed to fostering connections at Mindspace and to building a close-knit community in Frankfurt.

[Name] # Social Impact Lab Frankfurt

[Address]   Falkstraße 5, 60487 Frankfurt

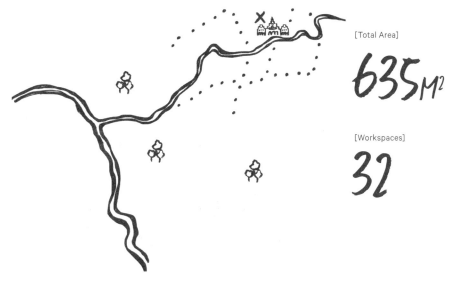

[Total Area]

635M²

[Workspaces]

32

[The Story]   Social Impact Lab is a nonprofit organization that was founded in 2011 with the express aim of bringing young migrants and social entrepreneurs together in the same space. In addition to Frankfurt, there are other Social Impact Labs across Germany, for example in Berlin, Hamburg, Munich and Stuttgart. Social Impact Lab Frankfurt, established in 2014, is located on the Bockenheimer Warte. The space serves predominantly as a program incubator (with programs AndersGründer and ChancenNutzer). Managing director Michael Wunsch says, "Without the programs, Social Impact Lab Frankfurt wouldn't exist, and it's the programs that predominantly finance the space." But the space also welcomes startups independent of the programs, so long as they're working towards the same values.

Inside is a bright, modern and spacious atmosphere with a selection of open desk spaces and more private rooms. The space also comes equipped with ample facilities for meetings, seminars, events and conferences for up to two hundred people. Michael considers Social Impact Lab to be more than just a space, and he happily points out the constant cross-pollination of ideas between startups, both independent and from the programs, as a good example: "We're not just offering facilities but more importantly we're a community where people can connect, seek help or offer help."

[Links]   Web: frankfurt.socialimpactlab.eu Facebook: socialimpactlabfrankfurt Twitter: @socialimpactlab

Face of the Space:
Birgit Heilig and Michael Wunsch have
supported social entrepreneurs for the last
four years. They cofounded the Social
Entrepreneurship Network Germany,
a lobby group for the German ecosystem,
in 2017. Since January 2018, they have
been the managing directors of Social
Impact Lab Frankfurt.

[Name] # WeWork Goetheplatz

[Address] Neue Rothofstraße 13–19, 60313 Frankfurt

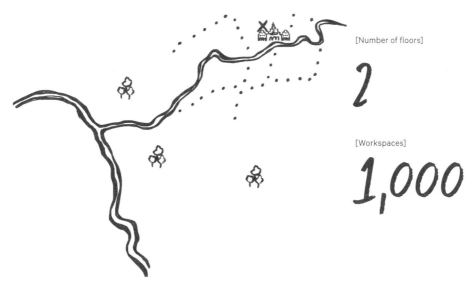

[Number of floors]

2

[Workspaces]

1,000

[The Story] WeWork Goetheplatz occupies two floors in an old office building near Goethestraße, one of the chic shopping streets in the Frankfurt city center. The decor is modern and fresh, and there's a variety of spaces to work that match all moods or energy levels. "It's like you're sitting at home with your family and friends in your living room," says Sabrina Haenle, WeWork's community manager. WeWork provides private offices ranging from one to fifty people as well as fixed and hot desks. The private offices are in demand among both startups and corporates, and the fixed and flex desk areas host a number of freelancers and consultants across industries, from business coaches to creative designers. "The companies really support each other to be more successful," says Sabrina.

The Goetheplatz location offers varying sizes of meeting rooms, with the largest holding up to twenty-five people, and also provides individual phone booths for calls. There's an indoor event space, an outdoor terrace for hosting barbeques, and a lounge on the first floor. Free coffee and tea are provided, and after 3 PM beer and locally produced *Apfelwein*, a typical Frankfurt drink, are on tap. Every Monday there is a TGIM (Thank God It's Monday) breakfast for members, and there are numerous networking and coaching events for members and non-members during the week.

[Links] Web: wework.com Facebook: WeWorkGermany Twitter: @WeWorkGermany

Face of the Space:
Sabrina Haelne joined WeWork as a community manager after a friend working for WeWork in Berlin recommended that she apply. She loves being able to work from a different space in the building every day, being surrounded by and speaking with many different people, and being able to bring her dog to work.

Dr. Gesine von der Groeben / BEITEN BURKHARDT

Partner and Lawyer of BEITEN BURKHARDT

From protecting your startup's intellectual property to learning all the necessary terms to understand and negotiate a successful investment deal, there will undoubtedly be a point in your entrepreneurial journey when you'll come face to face with complex legal issues. Oftentimes, founders have neither the experience nor expertise to make an informed decision in these situations, and that's where legal advice can help make things more comprehensible.

"When working with startups, I aim to educate and prepare them so they can go into negotiations with investors with a stronger sense of self-confidence, which they can only have if they understand the legal aspects of their deal. We explain difficult legal issues to them in a way that is easily understandable," says Dr. Gesine von der Groeben, partner and lawyer at BEITEN BURKHARDT, an independent German law firm that advises on all areas of commercial law. "Once entrepreneurs understand the legal terms, they can then evaluate their own needs more effectively and are in a better position to approach negotiations."

Founded in 1990 in Munich, BEITEN BURKHARDT has since grown to five offices across Germany and to international offices in Russia, China and Belgium. Currently, the firm consists of more than 292 lawyers covering an array of expertise as well as tax advisors and tax auditors worldwide. BEITEN BURKHARDT has a broad client base, including multinational companies, VC firms, business angels, banks, foundations, governments and startups.

As a member of the law firm's Startups & Venture Capital practice, Gesine advises startups at all stages (and from a variety of industries, such as fintech, food tech, mobility, gaming and medtech, among others) on financing rounds, exits, shareholder agreements, convertible loans and employees participation programs.

One of common mistake she sees entrepreneurs make when they're closing a funding round is that they're often so caught up in the amount of the deal that they don't think thoroughly about whether this specific kind of financing is the best option for their startup. "Instead of eyeing the figures, it's better to focus on what's important for the business," she says. "Think about the kind of investor your startup really needs."

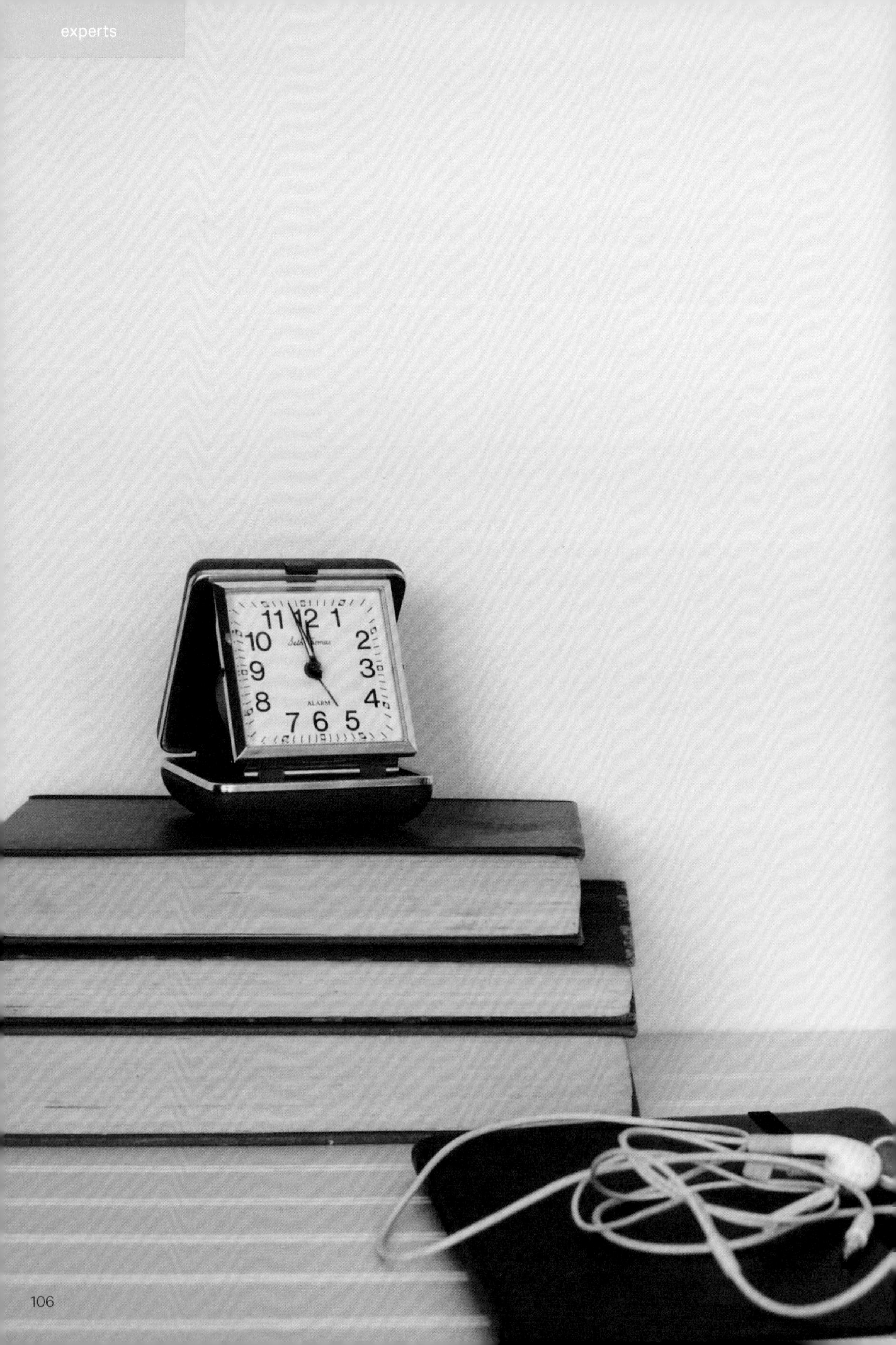
ALARM

Most important tips for startups:

- Understand what your IP is and make sure that it belongs to the company (and not to the founders). If the IP, which is one of the main assets of a company, belongs to an individual during a funding negotiation process, this can be a deal breaker for investors.

- Make sure to keep your cap table updated and organized at all times. Not only is a cap table interesting for investors, it's also important for a future exit. That's why it's crucial to ensure it's well structured and maintained regularly.

- Seek out legal advice early on to avoid any unpleasant (and expensive) surprises. Having a good legal structure in place from the start means your startup will save money overall in the long run. After all, it's always more expensive to ask a lawyer to help you after a problem has arisen.

For startups trying to navigate the financing process, Gesine has three pieces of advice to offer: First, protect your intellectual property (IP). "Make sure that the relevant IP is assigned to the company and not to the founders," says Gesine. "If the IP belongs to one of the founders or it's not protected properly while negotiating a deal, then the main asset is not with the company, and this could be a deal breaker for investors."

Creating a capitalization table (cap table) and managing it carefully is an important responsibility for founders. Since this is something that investors will certainly want to look at, Gesine believes it's critical for startups to always maintain a clean and well-structured cap table. Not only that: as a company grows, more stakeholders will receive shares, and it can get incredibly complex. "If you lose track of who has how many shares, this will impact a future exit," she says. "So take care of your cap table and maintain it regularly."

Finally, it's highly recommended to seek out good legal advice early on to avoid any expensive surprises in the future. "Having a proper legal structure from the very beginning is a preventative measure that reduces overall legal fees," says Gesine. "It's always more expensive to include a lawyer in the process after something has already happened. Saving pennies during early stages will cost dollars at exit. Shoddy set up and cavalier legal structure will inevitably surface during due diligence at exit or an IPO and have a tremendously negative impact on sales price or initial stock valuation."

To learn more about various aspects of commercial law, take a look at BEITEN BURKHARDT's blog (**beiten-burkhardt.com/en/news/blog**), which features articles on an array of legal topics written by lawyers and tax experts. "Ultimately, we want to be a trusted legal advisor for startups," says Gesine. "In addition to extensive legal experience across a number of sectors and an excellent network, we also offer barrier-free startup rates."

About

BEITEN BURKHARDT is a commercial law practice founded in Germany and active worldwide, with a range of expertise that covers all areas of commercial law relevant to our clients, whether listed companies, medium-sized companies, corporations, the public sector or startups. As a client, you will find more than just 292 strategically-thinking lawyers, tax advisors and auditors; you will also find 292 dedicated partners who have a special understanding of your matter and will work with you to develop individual solutions. Their integrated approach of law and tax advice provides short turnaround time and well-thought-out solutions from a dedicated advisor.

"Once entrepreneurs understand the legal terms, they can then evaluate their own needs more effectively and are in a better position to approach negotiations."

Sören Gahn and Aline Kubitza / Deutsche Bank

Head Startups@Germany - Central Region
Head Office Coordinator Startups@Germany

Launching and growing a startup can be exciting, but it's certainly not easy. Regardless of which stage you're in on the entrepreneurial journey, it requires a lot of time, hard work and constantly dealing with uncertainty. The team at Deutsche Bank knows this, which is why they rolled out special services to support startups of all sizes, from all industries, a couple of years back. Currently, Deutsche Bank's startup initiatives are available across Germany, with seven headquarters located in Frankfurt, Berlin, Hamburg, Cologne, Munich, Dusseldorf and Stuttgart.

"We help entrepreneurs in every stage of the startup life cycle with banking services as a well as various kinds of expertise and support, from seed stage to growth stage and expansion to new markets," says Sören Gahn, head of startups for the Central Region at Deutsche Bank. For early-stage startups, Deutsche Bank offers advice from experts, strategic support in developing business plans, and the opportunity to connect with key players in their global network, such as VCs, business angels, pitching platforms and financing partners. In the later growth and expansion stages, it provides assistance on growth financing, cash and currency management, and liquidity optimization, as well as advice on preparing for major milestones, such as an IPO, M&A or exit.

"We know that startups with scalable business models can grow very, very fast – often much quicker than mid-sized companies or corporates – and they have different needs. So we wanted to offer a different way to support them along their entire journey and cover their needs from a banking perspective," says Aline Kubitza, head office coordinator of Startups@Germany at Deutsche Bank.

Founders focused on scaling the business often find themselves overwhelmed by mounting to-do lists. Sören recommends getting support from experts as soon as possible to help solve the issues quickly and carve out a clear plan to scale. "As a growing startup, it's important to be clear about what you are doing and what you want to achieve," he says.

Not only that, running a startup is like a never-ending race against the clock, so be mindful of how you spend your time, especially when developing business strategies, searching for the right people for your team, outlining an organization structure and finding financing opportunities. "Time is money, so use your time efficiently," says Sören.

NEC | **DECEMBER** | DECEMBER | DEZEMBER

day.

20

Streda
Mittwoch

Čtvrtek
Thursday
Zimní slunovrat, první zimní den.
Natálie, Noel

51. 1

21

07

08

09

10

11

12

13

14

15

16

17

18

19

20

PROSINEC
DECEMBER

Most important tips for startups:

- **Be clear about what you're doing and how you plan to scale.** Having a good hard think about what you want to achieve with your startup will help you home in on the important tasks needed to drive your business forward.

- **Growing a startup is no easy task; get experts onboard ASAP to support you.** Whether it's advice on how to get funding or assistance with currency management, working with experienced professionals on specific areas will save you time overall so you can focus on building up the business.

- **Remember, time is money. Use your time efficiently.** Regardless of what task you're working on, it's crucial to careful with how you spend your time.

Deutsche Bank is a huge company, so entrepreneurs may not realize all the startup initiatives available. "In addition to the services offered to startups throughout each stage of their development," says Aline, "we have the Deutsche Bank Innovation Labs which scout for startup solutions to enlarge our product offer for clients as well as ideas that would improve our internal processes."

Located in Berlin, London, New York, Palo Alto, and Singapore, Deutsche Bank Innovation Labs (**labs.db.com**) seek out startups that are reimagining the world of fintech and connects them to decision-makers within Deutsche Bank (to create a culture of innovation).

In 2016, Deutsche Bank also unveiled the Digital Factory, a research and development center in Frankfurt for developing digital banking products for their customers. Over eight hundred software developers, financial experts and IT specialists work together in the Digital Factory with the aim of driving innovation and propelling the financial industry forward. There are also fifty workspaces designated for potential startup collaborators. One success story from the Digital Factory was the 'Deutsche Bank Mobile' app, which was created alongside a number of startups and marked the beginning of many more startup collaborations.

If you're a developer and not based in Frankfurt, then the dbAPI developer portal (**developer. db.com**) might be of interest. Through the application programming interface (API) you have the opportunity to use approved customer data to build digital products and services. Another way to catch the attention of Deutsche Bank is through its online Pitch Portal (**db.com/ company/de/pitch.htm**). There, startups and tech companies can fill in a form and pitch their solution, which will then be evaluated by the Deutsche Bank team on whether a collaboration is possible.

Have an exciting and innovative idea in the works? Don't hesitate to contact the Deutsche Bank team.

About

Deutsche Bank is Germany's leading bank, with a strong position in Europe and a significant presence in the Americas and Asia Pacific. It provides banking services to companies, governments, institutional investors, small and medium-sized businesses and private individuals. Against a backdrop of increasing globalization in the world economy, Deutsche Bank is very well-positioned, with significant regional diversification and substantial revenue streams from all the major regions of the world.

[Contact]   Email: **soeren.gahn@db.com** Telephone: **+49 (0) 69 910-24188**

[Links]   Web: **deutsche-bank.de/startups** Facebook: **DeutscheBankService**

"As a growing startup, it's important to be clear about what you are doing and what you want to achieve."

Eric Menges
/ FrankfurtRheinMain GmbH
International Marketing
of the Region

CEO and President of FrankfurtRheinMain GmbH International
Marketing of the Region

"Location, location, location." The phrase is often heard in the world of real estate to emphasize the importance of location in determining the value of a property; however, it also easily applies to entrepreneurs and growth companies, especially when it comes to choosing a place to start a business or set up a new office.

There are a number of factors to consider when selecting a location for your new business or company space, such as tax regulations, access to training or networking programs, affordable housing and ease of transportation. Not only that, it's also worth thinking about your company's planned growth and future space requirements.

"Office space is abundant in the Frankfurt Rhine-Main region," says Eric Menges, CEO and president of FrankfurtRheinMain GmbH International Marketing of the Region, an investment-promotion agency for the region. "It's high quality and low cost. And Frankfurt is a super international place, perhaps due to its long tradition of being a trade fair location where millions of people come from around the world every year, but also because of the financial services industry."

As the third largest metropolitan region in Germany, Frankfurt Rhine-Main refers to the area surrounding Frankfurt and covers more than 14,800 km2. The five biggest cities in this region are Frankfurt am Main, Darmstadt, Mainz, Offenbach and Wiesbaden.

When asked about the key benefits Frankfurt offers as a place for startups and later-stage companies, Eric responds, "For both the professional and private side of things, a key advantage is connectivity. Connection to and from the airport, as well as with the rest of Germany and Europe, is quick and easy. Even within the region, it hardly ever takes more than thirty minutes to get to the airport or another city in the area." This means that instead of spending tons of time commuting like in many cities around the world, you can use it to build up your business and focus on things that are important.

Most important tips for startups:

- **Reach out to governmental organizations or business promotion agencies for help when navigating a new startup scene.** These organizations can point you towards useful programs and contacts in the city or region, which you may not have found otherwise.

- **Get out and meet people.** With plenty of events and conferences happening through the region, there are many opportunities to network.

- **Take your time in deciding where to base your startup or scale your company.** Scope out different areas and offices, and make sure the business environment is a good fit for your needs before making the big decision.

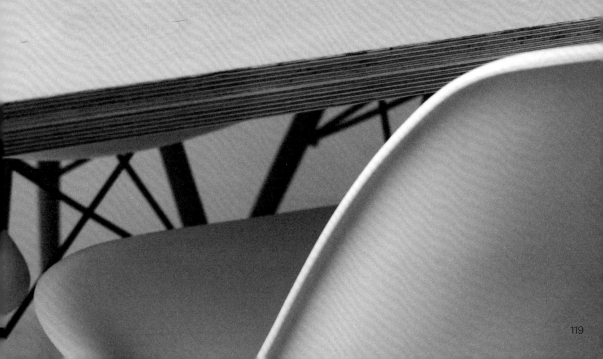

While many people see Frankfurt as a financial center, Eric says the region is home to an array of different industries that are often overlooked. "There are big names in IT, like Software AG and SAP, that have been here for a long time. In the pharmaceutical and life sciences space, there are major companies like Sanofi, Merck and Fresenius within the region. A lot of people don't realize it, but Frankfurt Rhine-Main is a big automotive hub, with large companies like Opel/PSA and Continental as well as several Asian car-makers setting up branches here."

For anyone thinking of Frankfurt as a place to launch a startup, scale a company or open a R&D center, Eric suggests that first you reach out to governmental initiatives or business promotion agencies, like FrankfurtRheinMain GmbH, that are keen on fostering the startup climate in an area. These organizations can guide you with everything from ways to get financing to finding special entrepreneurial support programs.

In addition to its Frankfurt am Main location, FrankfurtRheinMain GmbH has offices in London, Chicago, Shanghai and Pune for those that have questions or concerns about setting up shop in the region.

Second, engage with the local startup scene and make yourself known. "You need to be out and about at events and conferences, talking to people," Eric says. Expanding your network is crucial to the growth of your business, because it can help with connecting partners, acquiring customers, building a community and finding talent.

A good way to scope out some spots in the region before settling on a place is to check out some shared offices or coworking spaces in preferred areas. "Germany, unlike other European countries, is very decentralized. There are a range of industry clusters," says Eric. "Maybe you want to be close to universities or the banks, or the automotive industry. Regardless, it's worth looking around and exploring a bit before making a decision on where you want to base yourself. Take your time with finding the right place."

About

FrankfurtRheinMain GmbH International Marketing of the Region is the inward investment agency of Frankfurt Rhine-Main region. It's a company comprised of districts, towns and cities in the Frankfurt Rhine-Main region, and its task is to present and actively market the numerous strengths of the region. In addition, FrankfurtRheinMain GmbH implements targeted measures to position the region in the global competitive environment.

"It's worth looking around and exploring a bit before making a decision on where you want to base yourself."

David Eckensberger / Hessen Trade & Invest

Head of the International Affairs Department of Hessen Trade & Invest

Whether it's looking for the next round of funding or securing the next partnership, the challenges startups and growth companies face are more or less the same wherever you go. Increasingly, cities and regions are trying to make the lives of entrepreneurs easier by supporting them in various ways. Regardless of the stage and industry your company is operating in, this can be incredibly useful information when deciding on whether a location is a good fit for your next step.

"One of the biggest advantages about Frankfurt and Hessen as a location for startups and scale-up companies is its highly international business community. There are startup events happening every day and a pool of skilled talent coming from all over the world," says Dr. David Eckensberger, head of the International Affairs Department at Hessen Trade & Invest GmbH (HTAI), a governmental organization focused on strengthening the federal state of Hessen as a hub for economic and technological activity. Hessen has a population of more than six million people and is one of the economically strongest regions in Europe, with Frankfurt am Main being the biggest city in the area. This means there's no shortage of potential clients for startups and later-stage companies.

"Another asset we have is a strong infrastructure for entrepreneurs to tap into, which consists of incubators, accelerator programs, renowned universities, corporations and investors of all kinds," he adds. Let's not forget that Frankfurt is also well connected when it comes to transportation, with speedy connections to nearly every part of Europe and one of the most frequented airports in Germany and Europe. This is definitely a plus if you're the kind of founder who wants to expand your business across the region and will need to do a lot of traveling.

However, navigating a new place can be tough, especially if you're a budding entrepreneur looking to set up your business there. That's why HTAI is determined to help new startups get off the ground by connecting them to useful resources and offering various kinds of support – at no cost.

"We start by talking to the entrepreneurs to understand their business," says David. "Then we provide them with information that´s relevant to their market or industry and try to find the right contacts or communities in Hessen to connect them with, like our colleagues from the Technology & Innovation Department, for instance, who are excellent at networking." In addition, HTAI also offers hands-on workshops for participants who wish to learn specific innovation approaches, such as the lean startup methodology or design thinking.

 Most important tips for startups:

- When working on your startup, remember the Pareto principle, which states that 80 percent of your results come from 20 percent of your efforts. Accept the fact that you won't have a perfect product at the get-go, and keep developing it. It's all about getting your business started.

- Don't be afraid to ask for help. As an entrepreneur, time is of the essence. If you need guidance or support for something in particular, reach out to the many experts and consultants out there who are willing to help you out.

- Go out and network. Go to events, attend conferences, talk to people. There are so many opportunities in the Frankfurt Rhine-Main region. It's the best way to get connected to potential collaborators, investors and customers.

For scale-up companies that have a different set of needs, ranging from looking for growth financing to expanding to new markets, David says that Enterprise Europe Network Hessen (een-hessen.de) is highly useful for further support in this later stage of the entrepreneurial journey. Launched by the European Commission in 2008, the Enterprise Europe Network helps small and medium-sized enterprises gain know-how, innovate and internationalize as well as access EU funds. It's active in over sixty countries across the globe, and HTAI coordinates the support services in Hessen.

"Our experts can advise you on equity or funding, coach your company and help you find the right mentors or organize meetings and training sessions, and they can help you find the right partners abroad," David says of the many services offered by Enterprise Europe Network Hessen. "They can even come to your company to have a look at your innovation value chain, benchmark it and suggest measures to boost your innovation efficiency – all free of charge as part of our public support for enterprises."

For entrepreneurs working on a startup or scale-up, David has three general pieces of advice: First and foremost, he says to remember the Pareto principle, also known as the 80/20 rule, which suggests 80 percent of our results come from 20 percent of our efforts. Essentially, this is about how aiming for perfection can be an obstacle for success, especially in the early stages when it's highly likely that your product or service will change.

Next, don't be afraid to ask for help. "Keep in mind that you don't need to figure out everything on your own," says David. "There are a lot of experts and advisors who can help you grow your business. Their help can make a big difference – and save you so much time and money." Last but not least, get out there and network. Being active in the startup community and clearly communicating what you're doing is highly beneficial to your business. It can help bring new clients, potential partners and new opportunities for growth.

About

Hessen Trade & Invest GmbH (HTAI) is the economic development organization of the federal state of Hessen. It is tasked with continuing the sustainable development of Hessen as a business and technology location in order to consolidate and expand its competitiveness. Through targeted activities, HTAI contributes to maintaining and increasing the prosperity and living standard of all Hessian citizens in the long term. To achieve this, it partners with the business, scientific, administrative and political sectors.

" *Keep in mind that you don't need to figure out everything on your own. There are a lot of experts and advisors who can help you grow your business.* **"**

Barbara Sillich
/ KPMG AG

Partner, Tax Advice of KPMG AG

Pitching your startup at events, meetings and conferences is an important part of getting the word out about what your business does and why it's worth people's time. It also comes in handy when you're trying to convince talent or collaborators to hop onboard to help grow your company.

"It's absolutely essential for startups who often don't have many contacts in the very beginning to pitch themselves persuasively, whether it's to gain new clients and partners or to secure funding from investors and financial institutions," says Barbara Sillich, who is a partner in the Tax Advisory department at KPMG Frankfurt and also leads the Startup Business department in the region that covers Frankfurt, Mainz and Saarbrücken.

Being able to craft a compelling pitch for a particular audience is no easy feat. However, there are certainly ways to increase your chances of leaving a strong impression. One crucial thing to keep in mind when pitching is to keep it short and succinct. Remember, most people are strapped for time and don't have much patience for long explanations.

Barbara, who has been working with KPMG for eighteen years, says that she often comes across startups that need more than one minute to give their audience a gist of what they're about and what they stand for. "It's very important to be clear, concise and quick when explaining what your business does and stands for—and that can be very difficult."

That's why many pitch competitions often give founder participants a time-limit cap between one and five minutes to talk about what their startup is about. With such a short amount of time, it's critical to only include essential information, such as the problem you're solving, who your customers or users are, what makes it different from other similar products or services in the market, and why it's relevant now.

Another tip that Barbara has for entrepreneurs is to be passionate when pitching. If you're not excited about the product or service you're selling, it's likely the audience you're talking to also won't be super excited about it either. "Give us a feeling that you're burning for the idea," says Barbara. "The emotional part of a pitch is important in convincing others to invest in your startup or buy your product or service."

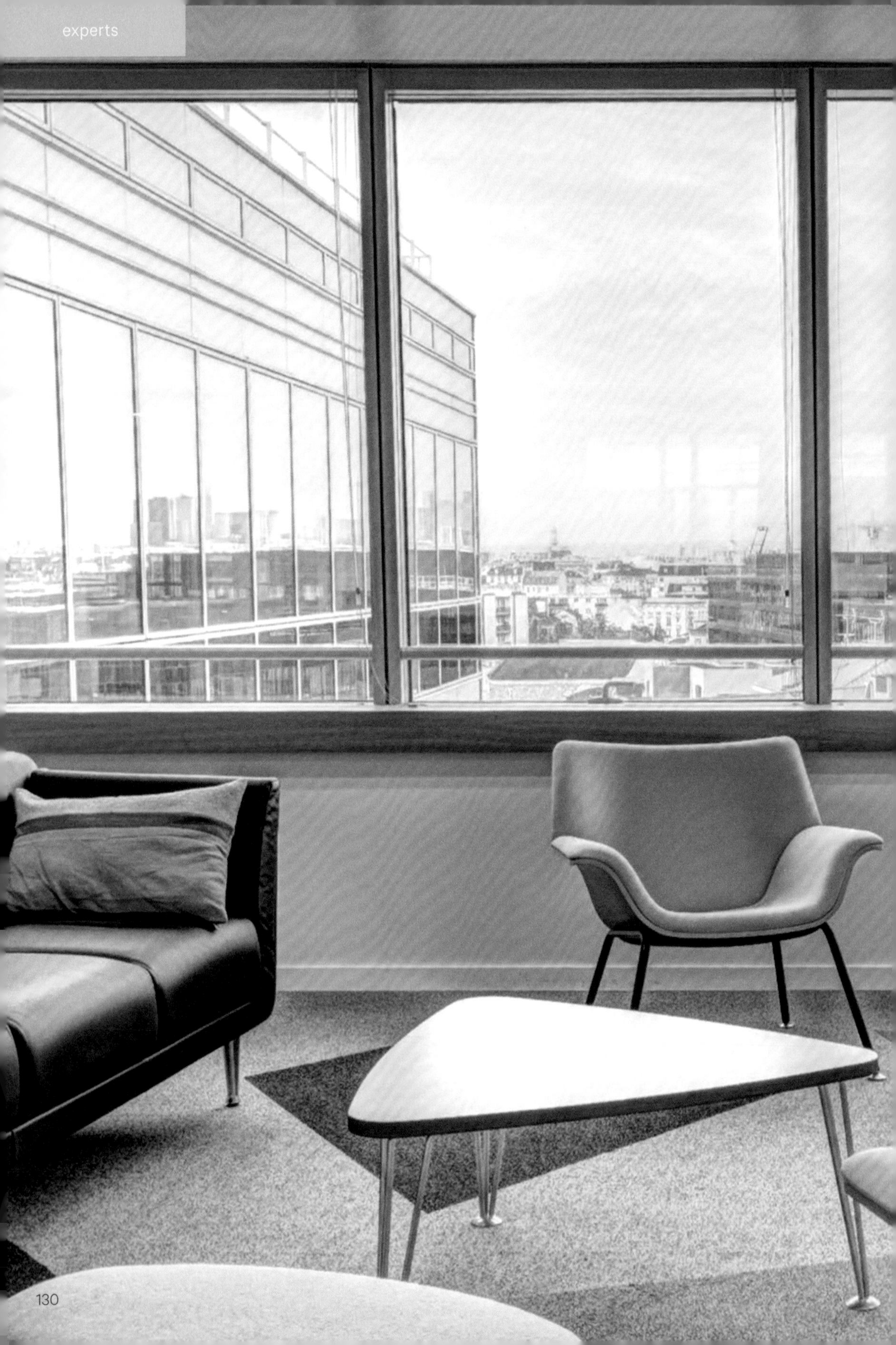

Most important tips for startups:

- **Make sure your pitch is short and succinct.** Remember that most people don't have much time or patience to listen to long explanations about what your startup does. Keep your pitch clear, concise and no longer than a couple of minutes, if possible.

- **Demonstrate how excited you are about what you're doing.** Being passionate about your startup idea is an important part of convincing investors to give you funding or convincing customers to buy your product.

- **Include tidbits about your startup's roadmap for the future.** Providing a peek into what your business strategy is, what's coming up next, and what your goals are in the next five or ten years is a good way to reiterate your startup's vision.

This doesn't necessarily mean you have to be super smooth in your presentation – not everyone is a natural when talking in front of an audience – it can simply mean being honest, engaging and letting your personality shine through when talking about your startup. People can usually gauge how authentic you are, so it's best to be yourself as much as possible (even if you have stage fright).

Finally, think about what your startup will look like down the line and include some tidbits about your vision in your pitch. "As a startup, there are so many things to do and sometimes entrepreneurs end up doing a little bit of everything," she says, "When pitching, founders need to focus on communicating the goals they want to pursue, what their vision is and what their business plan will look like in the future."

KPMG has a number of initiatives aimed at supporting startups. One of those is the Smart Start initiative (**hub.kpmg.de/smart-start-guide**), which consists of a specialized team that provides services on an array of topics (such as law, financing and HR) as well as business consulting to startups throughout their growth journey. Additionally, KPMG Frankfurt is a sponsor of the Hessischer Gründerpreis, a prize awarded to founders in the state of Hessen where KPMG also offers coaching to participants so they can improve their pitching technique.

For many startups, approaching such an established company like KPMG for advice might seem intimidating. However, Barbara highly encourages you to reach out to her if you need tax advice. And if you need support with another issue that KPMG might be able to help with, she can direct you to the right departments in the company. "Startups are very important clients to us," she says. "Remember that every big company started as a small company in the beginning."

About

In Germany, KPMG is one of the leading auditing and advisory firms and has around 10,700 employees at over twenty locations. Its audit services focuses on the auditing of consolidated and annual financial statements, the tax function incorporates the tax advisory services provided by KPMG, and its high level of specialist know-how on business, regulatory and transaction-related issues is brought together within its consulting and deal advisory functions.

[Contact]   Telephone: **+49 69 9587-2178**

[Links]   Web: **KPMG.de** Facebook: **KPMG** Twitter: **@kpmg** LinkedIn: **company/kpmg**

"It's very important to be clear, concise and quick when explaining what your business does and stands for."

Michael Gamber
/ Merck

Head of Merck Innovation Center

More and more, startups are working alongside corporates to achieve their mission. Each party offers the other something they need, and, together, they prop up each other's businesses. Larger firms are more experienced, have an extensive network and can offer valuable know-how. On the other hand, startups provide fresh ideas, speed and new ways of thinking. If it's the right pairing, this kind of partnership is a win-win strategy.

The Merck Innovation Center in Darmstadt aims to bring Merck employees, emerging startups and companies together under one roof to develop innovative technologies and businesses. In addition to a physical space that fosters creativity and idea exchange, the Innovation Center is home to Merck's Accelerator Program (**accelerator.merckgroup.com**), which offers selected startups three months of office space, access to Merck's internal and external network in sixty-six countries around the world, coaching from experts and up to €50,000 in financial support.

"Participating in the Accelerator Program at our Innovation Center can be an incredible opportunity for startups to boost their businesses and, at the same time, find a partner they can collaborate with. Perhaps it can even lead to their first deal with an established player," says Michael Gamber, Head of Innovation Center at Merck. "We're looking for partners that we can work together with in shaping the future."

Each year, Merck's Accelerator in Darmstadt invites up to ten startups working in the fields of healthcare, life sciences, performance materials or related fields (such as bio-sensing and interfaces, clean meat or liquid biopsy) to participate in its program. The program takes place at the headquarters in Darmstadt and startups from anywhere can apply.

Even after the Accelerator Program is over, Merck continues to support startups in their growth. Michael, who has been working on the concept of the Innovation Center since 2013, says the Accelerator continues to stay in contact with the startups and often helps advance conversations related to joint collaborations with Merck's internal teams, follow-up investments or R&D agreements.

Most important tips for startups:

- **Be open to partnerships with larger firms.** Landing funding from an investor isn't the only way to grow your startup these days. Teaming up with corporates can also boost your business. There are so many different ways to go about it. Be creative.

- **Finding the right partner is the key to a successful collaboration.** But in order to find the right partner, founders need to first reflect on what they want to achieve with their business, understand their own weaknesses and learn about what corporates are looking for.

- **Don't be afraid of failure.** As an entrepreneur, failure is simply part of the journey. Don't let it stop you from moving forward. Accept it, embrace it and learn from it.

Starting in 2019, some startups will get the chance to extend their Accelerator Program experience by going to Shanghai to be a part of Merck's China Innovation Hub Accelerator. Selection to participate in the China extension depends on how ready a startup is to enter the Chinese market as well as its potential to form local partnerships.

As for tips on leading a successful collaboration with larger organizations, Michael says it's important to be open to different kinds of partners from the get-go. When it comes to growth, some founders will only consider investors as a way to take their business to the next level. But, increasingly, teaming up with an established firm in your industry is proving to be an equally viable way to get a startup off the ground.

Finding the right partner for a collaboration is crucial, and this starts with understanding your own startup and its goals. "Get to know your business, identify your weak points and learn about what corporates need," says Michael. "At the Merck Innovation Center, we offer startups a top-notch training on a variety of useful topics, covering everything from human resources to finance and more. But perhaps what offers the most value is their interaction with our internal colleagues, who offer insights and expertise – and might become their future project partner."

Last but not least, "don't be afraid of failing," he says. As an entrepreneur, fear of failure can hold you back from a lot of opportunities, learning and growth. There's no doubt that failure is anxiety-inducing and painful, but it's important to remember that it's an inevitable part of the startup journey and often leads to new beginnings.

As for programs and initiatives in the Frankfurt Rhine-Main region, Michael says, "Supporting the Rhine-Main ecosystem is extremely important to us because only a dynamic ecosystem will attract the best startups. In the past, we collaborated with other accelerators through organizing a joint investor pitch event, supported entrepreneur roundtables, and sponsored some of the regional startup events around Darmstadt and in the Rhine-Main area." Currently, the Merck Innovation Center is exploring ways to offer more services and programs to startups in the region.

About

Merck is a leading science and technology company, active in healthcare, life science and performance materials. Since its establishment 350 years ago in Darmstadt, Germany, Merck has become truly global. Today, it has approximately 51,000 employees working on breakthrough solutions and technologies in sixty-six countries.

[Contact]   Email: **accelerator@merckgroup.com**

[Links]   Web: **accelerator.merckgroup.com** LinkedIn: **company/merck-group**

"Get to know your business, identify your weak points and learn about what corporates need."

Dr. Thomas Hain
/ Nassauische Heimstätte
/ Wohnstadt Group

Managing Director of Nassauische Heimstätte / Wohnstadt Group

When it comes to housing and urban living, technology is playing an increasingly bigger role, so it's no surprise that more and more startups and tech companies are trying to reimagine how we live and what city life means. However, working in this space is not without its challenges.

"The housing industry generally operates in very long cycles," says Dr. Thomas Hain, managing director of Nassauische Heimstätte / Wohnstadt Group, one of the leading housing and development companies in Germany. "When a new building is built, it usually takes twenty to thirty years before the next major investment takes place. This kind of decision-making process is a contrast to how startups work, in general. There are worlds between a corporate in the housing industry and a startup in any industry."

Fully aware of how the housing industry can be a difficult space to crack for entrepreneurs, Nassauische Heimstätte / Wohnstadt Group launched its hubitation accelerator program (hubitation.de) in March 2018, with the goal of supporting startups that want to reshape the future of housing and living in cities. Startups tackling the topic from different angles are welcome to apply, whether it's developing a solution for smart homes and urban planning or designing concepts for residential architecture and efficient energy use in a living space.

Hubitation consists of a mentorship program and a contest, and aims to combine innovative ideas with the know-how that the Nassauische Heimstätte / Wohnstadt Group has garnered since its founding nearly one hundred years ago. "The startup scene seems to be saturated with money and investors, so we wanted to focus on developing pilot projects with the hubitation accelerator program," says Thomas. Each year, hubitation calls for startups to submit ideas for its contest (hubitation.de/contest). Winners receive access to the company's extensive network as well as the opportunity to collaborate on a pilot project together.

Most important tips for startups:

- **The housing and urban-living space is a tough sector to break into, so reach out to corporates and larger organizations early on to garner support for your idea.** Don't forget that established organizations in the industry have the resources and network to help you scale your startup. Why not try teaming up with one of them to fulfil your vision?

- **Be aware that partnering with corporates means adapting to a different pace of working.** It's a well-known fact that corporations take a bit more time to make decisions than startups do. Take this into consideration and remember that both parties are working towards one goal: reshaping the future of housing and living in cities.

- **When it comes to branding and marketing, be authentic.** Developing a marketing strategy that's line with your vision and values is crucial to maintaining the integrity of your product.

In order to break into the housing and urban living space, Thomas believes that it's crucial for startups to reach out and collaborate with corporates early on. Even if you have a visionary idea, it needs to be understood by the market and strategically executed – and larger organizations have the network and resources to help out with that.

However, working with corporations means moving at a different kind of pace, which can be a tough balancing act for entrepreneurs who are often told to "move fast and break things" by the startup world. Thomas understands this dilemma. "On the one hand," he says, "founders need a lot of patience and tact in order not to overwhelm corporates. On the other hand, the industry expects and needs a lot of unconventional ideas, rapid testing and new solutions for challenges that may not yet be apparent to us today." It's crucial to be aware of this dynamic and bear in mind that the right partnership will benefit both parties equally. "All beginnings are difficult. There is no difference here between startups and corporates."

Finally, when it comes to marketing and promoting your startup, don't forget about staying true to your vision and values. "From my point of view, authenticity is very important," says Thomas, "While marketing and product placement are certainly necessary and helpful to the business, it always come back down to the quality and integrity of your idea and product."

Currently, Nassauische Heimstätte / Wohnstadt Group supports innovators and startups by offering mentoring and a contest through its hubitation accelerator. Looking ahead, Thomas says that the company aims to do more collaborations with universities and entrepreneurial organizations to boost their engagement in the startup community. "We're still learning here," he says. "So if there are any ideas from the community on how to improve hubitation, we're very open to that and would be happy to hear from startups."

About

Nassauische Heimstätte / Wohnstadt Group is one of the leading German housing companies: with around 60,000 apartments in around 140 locations. It has built around 180,000 apartments in ninety-five years. The company's social mission is to supply broad sections of the population with affordable housing. Every day, more than 730 employees work for Nassauische Heimstätte / Wohnstadt Group's tenants and neighborhoods.

[Contact]   Email: contest@hubitation.de Telephone: +49 (0) 60 6069 1589

[Links]   Web: hubitation.de Facebook: hubitation Twitter: @hubitation Instagram: hubitation

"While marketing and product placement are certainly necessary and helpful to the business, it always comes back down to the quality and integrity of your idea and product."

Jonas Lorson
/ R+V Insurance

Head of Strategy & Innovation of R+V Insurance

If you're an entrepreneur with an interesting solution for the insurance sector, now's your time to shine. Insurers are beginning to recognize that emerging technologies are changing the way they interact with their customers and operate within the industry.

"A couple of years ago, the insurance industry wasn't as open to working with startups," says Jonas Lorson, head of Strategy and Innovation at R+V Insurance, one of the biggest insurance companies in Germany. "In the past two years, attitudes have changed and people in the industry are now keen on collaborating with startups."

According to a report by global strategy and consulting company Accenture, the number of investments in the insurance technology (insurtech) industry increased 39 percent globally in 2017, with the total value of deals reaching $2.3 billion. Although North America is spearheading the growth in terms of number of deals and total value, the number of deals in Europe grew 118 percent, with the total value reaching $679 million, which makes it an up-and-coming insurtech hub.

Cracking the insurance industry is no easy feat, though. "Insurance is a very low-engagement product," says Jonas. "Nobody wakes up in the morning and says, 'Today is the day I finally buy my new insurance.'" That's why he thinks it's important for entrepreneurs to think about how to create awareness about the product and increase engagement among customers. Another challenge is that insurers often offer a range of products that can be rather complex. That's why Lorson is adamant that "one-size-fits-all" solutions don't work in this industry.

One area that the insurance sector can definitely improve on is the digitalization of documents and contracts. "Our industry is driven by information, which is good, but much of this information is still on paper. This could be something that a startup can tackle."

Jonas and his team are responsible for coordinating innovation initiatives with R+V Insurance, a company that has more than fifteen thousand employees. "Our team reaches out to startups and organizations for potential collaborations. We act as a sort of bridge between third-party companies and our internal innovators," he says. Based on his experience working in the insurance industry, Jonas has a couple of pieces of advice for entrepreneurs trying to break into the world of insurtech.

Most important tips for startups:

- Focus on doing one thing better than anyone else rather than on doing multiple things at once. Having a clear idea about what your business model is and what value proposition you want to create can be a way to stand out from the crowd.

- When pitching to corporates, remember that they make decisions on a different timeline than startups. After connecting to a corporate, be patient and give them time to decide. Just because they don't reply immediately, it doesn't mean they're not interested; it might just take a bit more time.

- Land a partnership with an insurer as soon as you can to build credibility within the industry. Because the insurance sector is still quite conservative and risk-averse, having a deal with an insurer (it doesn't have to be with one of the big guns) will help you get the attention of others in the industry.

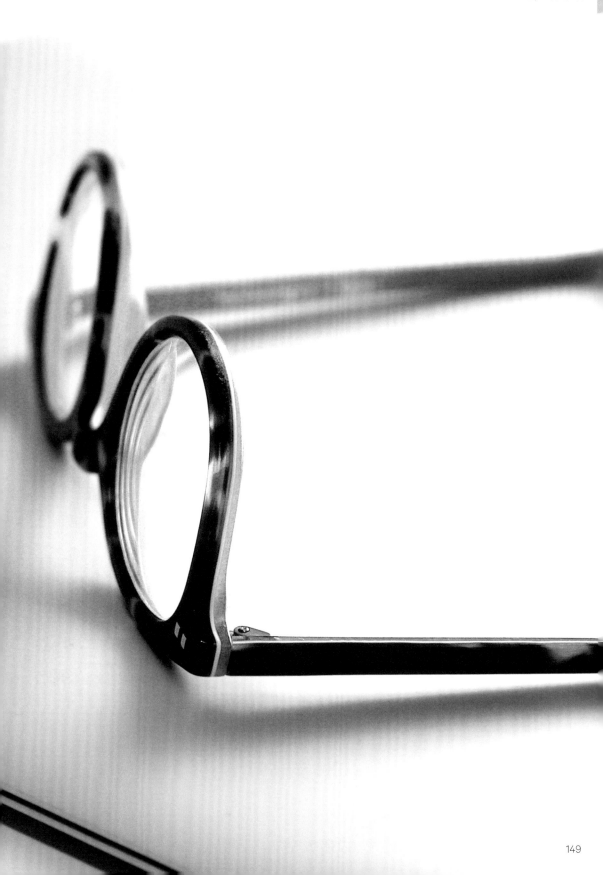

First, instead of trying to do too many things at once, focus on doing one thing better than anyone else. "Having a clear idea about what your business model is and what value proposition you want to create will help us differentiate your solution from others and, in my opinion, will lead to success."

When approaching corporates for collaborations, bear in mind that larger organizations likely have a different timeline than what you as a startup have in mind. In other words, patience is virtue in these situations. "After connecting to a corporation, give them time to think," says Jonas. "Oftentimes, startups expect a quick answer and can get a bit insecure if they don't hear back within one or two weeks. However, it might take more time than that for a corporate to make a decision."

Another thing to remember is that the insurance industry is still rather conservative. This means that most traditional insurers are on the risk-averse side when considering collaborations, especially since their core business is about managing risk. "I would suggest closing your first deal with a partner as soon as possible," says Jonas. "It doesn't have to be with a big insurer, but once you've secured one deal, it'll help you get the attention of the bigger players."

R+V Insurance is actively involved in startup ecosystems across Germany. In Frankfurt, the team participates in events at the startup space and community TechQuartier regularly. The company is also a founding member of InsurLab Germany, a hub in Cologne that promotes insurtech innovation. In addition to its own internal innovation lab, dubbed "MO14," R+V insurance is open to meeting startups working in the insurance space, regardless of what stage they're at.

"Our approach to innovation is always evolving," says Jonas. "We're always open to engaging and collaborating with third parties. At the moment, we don't have strict processes for this. We assess every single opportunity and then decide what to do."

About
R+V Insurance is one of the market leaders in the German insurance industry. It is the insurance unit of the number-one cooperative financial services network of Volksbanken and Raiffeisenbanken in Germany, serving more than thirty million clients. The premium income of R+V was more than €15.3 billion in 2017.

"*Having a clear idea about what your business model is and what value proposition you want to create will help us differentiate your solution from others.*"

Ann Rosenberg
/ SAP Next-Gen

Senior Vice President and Global Head of SAP Next-Gen

"It's time to activate your inner science-fiction imagination," says Ann Rosenberg, senior vice president and global head of SAP Next-Gen. Originally from Denmark and now based in New York, Ann works to support purpose-driven innovation platforms and networks all over the world, and has introduced the concept of science-fiction thinking into startup and corporate development, in part to unlock the potential of tech people and to reimagine how a sustainable future can be achieved. This is in line with SAP's commitment to support the seventeen Global Goals for Sustainable Development.

Set up in 2015 by world leaders from UN member states, the Global Goals aim to create a better future by 2030, namely by striving to reach goals such as eradicating poverty, ending hunger, achieving gender equality and ensuring good health and quality education for everyone. With SAP Next-Gen, Ann and her team work alongside a global network of researchers, accelerators, companies, startups, thought leaders and partners to support entrepreneurs and innovators in developing forward-thinking and impactful solutions to problems impacting not only the future, but the present as well.

Both on the local scale in Frankfurt and on the world stage, Ann and the SAP Next-Gen program aim to educate innovators to exponentially develop tech, so that by 2030 many of the Global Goals may be met. Frankfurt is linked to the innovation hub around SAP's global headquarters in Walldorf.

SAP Next-Gen creates connections between promising startups and corporates who may benefit from forward-thinking collaboration. Ann suggests that startups as well as corporates take responsibility for their technological innovations and create movements, and she urges entrepreneurs to use their know-how to solve the world's problems. "People don't just want to buy products," she says. "You need your purpose embedded into your business. It's not just about a great idea, it's also about driving purposeful impact."

Most important tips for startups:

- Activate your science-fiction thinking and imagination to unlock the potential of exponential technologies to enable positive social change. The future is coming fast and having a positive impact on the world either as a startup or a corporate means understanding how technology can be an enabler for good.

- Lead with purpose, in line with the seventeen Global Goals. Being purpose driven will make you more future-proof and more focused on your vision. Represent a diverse range of talent to support the people-oriented parts of the Global Goals.

- Take the stage; start a movement. Startups and corporate enterprises that succeed are also driving communities and movements. Create networking opportunities and collaborative spaces for your movement to take shape and flourish.

- Connect with the Frankfurt chapter of SAP Next-Gen. Frankfurt is a hub of financial business, emerging startups, and strong educational programs. Look to create B2B solutions and innovations leveraging the SAP Next-Gen community in Frankfurt.

Such a business philosophy is bolstered by Ann's initiative to use science-fiction thinking to inspire startups and corporates via workshops and talks. She has even written a book on science-fiction thinking in innovation, entitled *Science Fiction - A Starship for Enterprise Innovation*. In the book, she quotes *Harvard Business Review* writer Eliot Peper as saying, "Science fiction isn't useful because it's predictive. It's useful because it reframes our perspectives on the world... It creates space for us to question our assumptions." If you want to be successfully purpose driven, you can call upon science-fiction narratives to help you see where your technology may lead you. As prolific science-fiction author Ursula K. Le Guin said, "Science fiction is not prescriptive; it is descriptive."

"Science fiction's proven track record of envisioning the future is one reason we are confident that science-fiction thinking can serve as a wellspring for purposeful innovation and for an enterprise's ongoing transformation into an intelligent enterprise," Ann says. "The difference between those groundbreaking innovations and the ones that are making our lives better now and in the years to come is the process of their genesis, a process we call Innovation 4.0."

Innovators hoping to have a positive impact on the future through accelerating solutions to the Global Goals can utilize the methodology behind Innovation 4.0, which is the outcome of bringing together the Global Goals with exponential technology and science-fiction thinking. One such application, Ann says, is integrating voice into app development, uniting a great tech idea with a concept from science-fiction narratives.

"In today's business world, we work under the assumption that technology now enables us to achieve any outcome we imagine," says Ann. "Technology becomes an enabler for good, for the enterprises and the people who manage, shape and drive them." Science-fiction thinking helps us to envision how powerful technology can be used for higher social purposes, and it can help innovators examine how their current work can support bringing about a sustainable future.

About

SAP Next-Gen is a purpose-driven innovation university and community aligned with SAP's commitment to the seventeen UN Global Goals for sustainable development. The community leverages 3,600+ educational institutions in 116 countries, 130+ SAP Next-Gen labs/hubs at universities and at partner and SAP locations, 100+ SAP Next-Gen Chapters, a growing global network of 40+ Girls' Lounges at campuses, as well as entrepreneurs, accelerators, tech community partners, venture firms, futurists and purpose-driven institutions. The aim is to reimagine the future of industries and the intelligent enterprise; seed in disruptive innovation with startups; build skills for digital futures; and use new mindsets such as science-fiction thinking and initiatives such as #sheinnovates to accelerate "Innovation with Purpose" linked to the SDGs.

[Contact]   Email: **ann.rosenberg@sap.com**

[Links]   Web: **sap.com/next-gen** Facebook: **SAPNextGen** Twitter: **@SAPNextGen**

"It's time to activate your inner science-fiction imagination."

Julian Weste
/ Wirecard

VP, Financial Institutions and Fintech for Europe and the US of Wirecard

Dismissing the importance of payment solutions is one of the biggest mistakes a startup can make, according to Julian Weste. "Every startup hopes to earn money," Julian says. "But if you want to earn money and be paid, you need help building infrastructure which is as efficient, secure and convenient as possible." While payment might seem like a challenge throughout a founder's entrepreneurial journey that's far from exciting, it's crucial. You may have the greatest idea in the world, but if no one can buy what you're selling and you haven't carefully considered how money from your customers can get into your account, the survival of your startup will be at risk, Julian says.

In his current role at Wirecard, Julian is responsible for leading teams that take care of new and established customers alike in areas such as sales and account management. These customers include banks, financial institutions, e-money institutions and organizations that need licenses. Having worked with a wide range of fintech companies since he joined Wirecard in 2015, many of which have been startups, Julian has seen many founders fail to do their research when it comes to seeking out a payment solutions provider. One of the typical mistakes they make is they don't weigh out their options, he says. As well, startups often disregard the significance of having a provider which prioritizes innovation, a crucial aspect in the fast-changing payment environment.

One way in which Wirecard ensures that it drives innovation, such as in the digitalization of payments, is by taking on new customers. "Since we onboard customers on a regular basis, including well-known fintech companies, we're always learning and gaining knowledge about new technologies," Julian says. Startups in Wirecard's roster of customers include Berlin-based banking app Kontist, payment card Curve and digital banking service Holvi. Wirecard's other customers include Twisto, awarded as "Best European Payments & Transfers Company 2017" by European FinTech Awards 2017, and Spendit, a multi-award-winning HR and fintech company.

Most important tips for startups:

- **Choose a payment solutions provider that speaks the same language as you.** Seek out a provider which truly understands what you're looking for and is most suitable for your startup.

- **This provider should moreover have cutting-edge technology.** Working with a provider that's at the forefront of digitalization is important so that they can help you in a comprehensive way.

- **Lastly, consider the importance of global reach. Instead of selecting a provider that's only based in your local area, choose one that operates globally.** This will likely come in handy further down the line when your startup starts to grow internationally.

If you decide to work with Wirecard, you'll have the newest and best technology as well as the full range of payment methods available to you, according to Julian. Seeking out a provider with cutting-edge technology that your startup can benefit from is paramount for your business, he says. Another piece of advice Julian has for startups is to consider a provider that speaks the same language as you. In other words, they should have a deep understanding of what your needs are and what you're looking for. Having a provider that operates internationally, rather than just regionally, is also necessary. "Most startups want to expand to other countries at some point," Julian says. In light of this possibility, founders can avoid having to look for new suppliers, create new contracts and observe new laws simply by opting for a provider which has global reach. With entities in the US, Asia and elsewhere, Wirecard can support startups in terms of growth by consulting them on which payment methods to use in which country as well as the handling of different currencies.

Since it launched just under two decades ago in 1999, Wirecard has grown significantly. Now, as one of the largest fintech companies in Germany and a global player with around 5,000 employees worldwide, it is a startup success story in and of itself. In spite of this, Julian emphasizes that Wirecard still values working with, supporting and consulting fintech startups. "We have to stay in touch with smaller businesses in order to be innovative," he says. "Despite our large size, we're not like other companies that have grown and are only in touch with big companies, so don't be afraid of getting in touch with us."

About

Listed on the German stock exchange since September 2018, Wirecard AG specializes in payment processing and issuing. Headquartered in Bavaria, the technology group is a full-service provider and operates primarily B2B. Although Wirecard is a leader on the global stage for its software and IT, the company works closely with startups and aims to constantly expand its portfolio with innovative payment technologies.

[Contact]   Email: **fintech.europe@wirecard.com**

[Links]   Web: **wirecard.com** Facebook: **wirecardgroup** Twitter: **@wirecard**

"If you want to earn money and be paid, you need help building infrastructure which is as efficient, secure and convenient as possible."

ders

Corinna Haas

Cofounder / INGA

After working at one of the world's largest banks for eleven years in graduate recruiting, Corinna Haas left the company with the goal of reinventing the way the job market sees human resources. On her journey, she met two like-minded souls in Francisco Otto and Kim Körber, and in 2017, two years after she'd left the bank, they founded INGA together. INGA, with the tagline "Your Social Recruiting Bot," was created as a solution not just for medium-sized businesses to attract the right talent but also for talent to find their dream job. Corinna and her team aspire to simplify the recruiting process and free up space for HR people to spend valuable time with applicants and employees. On this mission, she focuses on working with early-stage startups, combining their flexible approach with processes and structures to reach a higher level of professionalism.

Can you first tell us about the company and how the solution works?
INGA builds a bridge between companies and talents and minimizes the effort for both sides in the recruiting process using social media channels and chatbot conversations. For the company, it takes only thirty minutes to brief INGA with all relevant criteria and expectations for the role, presenting the benefits the company offers to new employees. We then create a social media campaign under our brand "Traumberufe - Wechseln macht glücklich" and can reach a specific target group of people potentially suitable for and interested in such a position. For the talent, all it takes is a brief chat with the INGA chatbot to see if the position and employer are of interest and to submit a short application without the need to upload a CV. For both sides, it's an effective and time-saving process to learn about each other and get in contact for a further assessment.

Can you give us an example of INGA in action?
INGA works especially well for "hidden champions" with a weak employer brand, such as small or non-existing recruiting or HR teams in rural areas doing B2B business. For example, we worked with a successful company that manufactures machines for the packaging industry. They urgently needed service technicians as their order books were full to the brim. We worked closely with the co-head of service and delivered candidates quickly so that within three weeks, he could contact the promising candidates via phone and make two offers. This is an ideal case example of how efficient recruiting can be achieved with a direct approach.

What inspired you to found INGA, given your background in corporate recruiting?

I learned a lot from the corporate world, especially the importance of having the right processes and structures in place and how those same processes are sometimes slow to adapt to new developments in the labor market, such as adapting to the desire for impact, meaningfulness, work-life balance and room to maneuver in the workplace – not just in Generation Y and Millennials but also in Gen-X employees. Often, the application process of big corporations is well designed for the needs of a huge recruitment machine but not necessarily for the needs of the applicants. Why should someone spend one to two hours filling in online forms and uploading a CV, motivation letter and transcripts if the outcome is more than uncertain given the large number of candidates applying for the same role? And will the recruiter even take the time to screen applications properly? As a recruiter and HR person myself, I'm passionate about working with humans, getting to know them, and learning about their interests, qualifications and development areas, and their potential for a specific role and fit to the company and team culture. I always wished for a tool that would free up my time for such qualitative HR work by automating all those repetitive screening steps that could easily be done by software. And that is what we offer with INGA.

Is there anything you wish you could change about HR?

I wish that HR people had more time to actually find, develop and retain the right talents within their company instead of spending a lot of time on administrative tasks. In many companies, the recruiting process is still very manual, as CVs or online applications are being evaluated by a person regarding the basic prerequisites a potential candidate needs to have for a certain role. Those could be a required level of education, experience in a specific area, language skills and so on. This pre-selection can be automated, so that the recruiter has more time to actually interview and interact with the candidate in person.

Next would be the onboarding process, which includes all the documents and information needed to get the new team member started as an employee, followed by the planning of the first days and weeks within the firm in terms of meeting relevant coworkers, learning about the organization, and the tech-set up. Part of this can be automated as well so that the HR person can focus on real interaction with the new employee. And this approach could continue within every step of the employee lifecycle. I also do not like the term "Human Resources" and would rather see it renamed in and developed towards "People and Organization."

" As clients often feel more comfortable with the old ways, it's your task to present new solutions to them and make them understand the value. "

Can you tell us about some of your early struggles?

Keeping your focus on the important and relevant stuff is sometimes difficult. Having the opportunity to create the "ideal company and workplace culture" that my team and I have always envisioned, parallel to permanently improving the product, understanding the need of both the talents and the companies, coming up with a suitable pricing model, creating a sales process, setting up the right communication systems internally, making the clients happy, enlarging the monthly revenues and having a good work-life-blending is a constant juggling of priorities and focus.

Can you speak about your best decision so far?

Back when we started, the three of us were all working as consultants, and we started INGA as a side project, so we all gave roughly 20 percent of our time. From day one, we had paying customers plus a functioning product, and we soon realized that only giving a fifth of our time to the project was not enough as we saw the huge potential of INGA. So we decided to "go all in" in June 2018, and that was the best decision, because since then we've grown to a team of nine (as of November 2018) and have moved into a coworking space in the center of Frankfurt, and we're talking with potential investors for a pre-seed round, have been part in several pitch competitions and are working on becoming a full tech startup.

Is there anything you wish you'd known before starting the company?

We should have trusted the algorithm earlier. We're using machine learning to optimize our ads in social media channels, and in the beginning we tried to improve the campaigns manually, but we learned quickly that we can trust the machine. On a more personal note, I underestimated the time and effort one is willing to invest in creating such a startup and seeing your vision come to life. Constantly having the best of INGA in mind and working for a larger goal can take a toll. It took me a while to understand that charging my own batteries is important for the long run, so now I meditate each morning and try to squeeze in some yoga once or twice a week into my busy schedule.

Is there any advice you'd like to give up-and-coming startups?

When developing your product, do test quickly, use the feedback to improve the product and then test the improved version in a speedy way. Do not overthink, but remember to get stuff done. "Better done than perfect" helps you to focus on the solutions that actually work best for the client as you get instant feedback, but don't implement all the requests of clients without questioning them, as you want to change the world and this needs new approaches and new ideas. As clients often feel more comfortable with the old ways, it's your task to present new solutions to them and make them understand the value. Become professional in your structures and processes quickly, as this builds trust and raises efficiency. And always keep your vision in mind: don't lose the focus on why you're actually doing what you're doing.

What can you say about starting up in the Frankfurt region?

I view Frankfurt as very influenced by the banks, consultancies and lawyers and thus see a certain seriousness about how startups are also evolving. Founders in the Frankfurt area seem to be quite thoughtful about getting started and find a growing ecosystem of meetups, coworking spaces, networking events and events initiated by city officials and also an active group of business angel investors. I just moved to Frankfurt in August 2018 after living fifteen years in Mainz; the startup scene in Mainz is also growing, and I like the collaboration within the Rhine-Main area. I actually like that the scene is still rather small, as the connections I made with other founders, networkers and others have been quite intense and have helped me immensely in first developing my consulting business for startups and then actually finding my cofounders.

[About]   INGA is a social recruiting platform dedicated to matching the best talent to the right jobs. The company uses social media to attract candidates, and an AI chatbot to engage them for brief conversations before committing to job applications. INGA's recruitment process saves time and energy for both applicants and human resources people, allowing for more qualitative work whilst automating repetitive processes.

[Links]   Web: inga.one Facebook: halloinga Twitter: @halloinga

What are your top work essentials?
A MacBook Pro, iPhone X, internet
and human interaction.

At what age did you found your company?
Forty-two.

What's your most-used app?
Facebook, Slack, Trello, Pomodoro and Headspace.

**What's the most valuable piece of advice
you've been given?**
Better done than perfect.

What's your greatest skill?
I always see the positive side of things, situations
and people. The glass is always full.

Daniel Putsche

Founder and CEO / Candylabs

Daniel has his roots in digital consulting as a project lead for neckermann.de and Publicis, where he also gained valuable experience in Silicon Valley. Back in Germany, he cofounded and led a software offshoring company for more than two years before cofounding Candylabs, a digital consulting company, in 2013. In addition, he has founded other exciting projects and startups and is booked for keynote speaking engagements. Daniel has expertise in digital technologies, venture building and business models, as well as entrepreneurship and startup methods.

Could you please describe your entrepreneurial journey and your initial idea when you founded Candylabs?

I started my career as a project lead at a company called **neckermann.de**, a mail-order company trying to transform itself into an e-commerce company. With the idea to broaden my horizons, I moved on from being a consultant to working at Publicis after four years. While at Publicis, I also had the chance to work in San Francisco, and here I met some players in the local startup scene. I was at an event called Vator Splash and there were some guys on stage I'd never heard of – they were Dick Costolo and Peter Thiel. When I was at home that evening, I started Googling these guys, and this was essentially my starting point as an entrepreneur.

I came back to Germany, ended my contract at Publicis and started my first company, which happened to be a software-offshoring company. Two years and many valuable lessons later, I decided to quit and start Candylabs. There was no exceptional business idea behind Candylabs, but it was rather about resetting myself as an entrepreneur. Candylabs grew from doing software development to being a successful company that helps established organizations in pulling off new digital ventures. My most important lesson as an entrepreneur is that it's not about the idea but about the operational excellence in executing the idea. And that also means that the customer is shaping your product.

Is there a best practice your company follows?

There is no specific single best practice, as we cover kind of the whole supply chain in optimizing, transforming and developing disruptive digital business models. But, a topic which often results in interesting measures and findings for corporates is the validation of business models or product ideas using a method we named "virtual prototyping." Through this method, we create and validate ideas for our customers apart from their usual customer relations and with low risks, costs and effort but with real market data. This enables us to gain a lot of experience and speed in enhancing our expertise. In the usual corporate structure, most innovative ideas would have little to no chance to survive and would be crushed at the very first instance due to structural circumstances. In contrast to this, we can deliver quick results, provide exciting insights, and put the organization in a position to make innovation decisions based on data.

What was one of your early challenges while starting up and how did you overcome this?

Regardless of which founder I talk to or which business I founded, it never turned out to be an easy or smooth ride. It was the same for me when I founded Candylabs. To be honest, there was no single obstacle that made starting up tough but rather the combination of small and plentiful challenges I needed to solve, from closing deals to finding the right team to acquiring funds. If you need to cope with all these topics at the same time, you're going to struggle. We overcame these challenges by allowing ourselves to have slower growth and attempting to solve each issue one by one. "We," by the way, is one of the major reasons why we were able to survive in the early stages: being two founders helped us get more done with a higher quality. I would always try to start a business together with a cofounder moving forward.

What's one of your biggest entrepreneurial mistakes to date?

During the transition from my previous company to Candylabs, I learned a lot about non-compete clauses as a shareholder. Eventually, I had to spend some serious money to get into a position to be able to start Candylabs. But, being honest about your mistakes and failures allows room for personal and professional growth. Referring to my biggest or my most expensive mistake so far, I would never accept a post-contractual non-compete clause on a shareholder level again.

What's been your best decision to date as an entrepreneur?

It's less a decision I made as an entrepreneur and rather the decision I made in order to become an entrepreneur. As an entrepreneur, you must accept life being a rollercoaster to get the long-term results. This is what I like and live for.

"My most important lesson as an entrepreneur is that it's not about the idea but about the operational excellence in executing the idea."

Are there things you wish you'd known before becoming an entrepreneur? If yes, what would you have done differently?

It's a bit like having kids, isn't it? If you'd have known before what it really meant to stay up all night and then go to work the next day and try to get things done, maybe you'd have thought twice about it in the first place; but whatever downside you experience, you believe your kids and family are the most precious things in your life – and nearly the same goes for me when talking about being a founder. If I'd have known before how difficult it was going to be, I might have never started a business; however, today I cannot imagine doing anything other than being a founder.

Do you have any recommendations for young entrepreneurs or startup founders?

Something I put less focus on at the very beginning of Candylabs was a deep analysis of the market and the needs of our customers. We knew that technological progress and the speed of change was going to be a topic in the future, and this was one of the reasons to found Candylabs, but it took us more than three years to really identify the challenges of our customers and build products that allow them to deliver new ventures and business models, even in complex environments. Sure, it's part of the B2B game; however, when founding new companies or ventures, we put a lot of focus on the market opportunity as well as current and future user and customer needs. Focusing on these things will help every founder get more early-stage traction.

With whom would you like to work together with for one day and why?

Dara Khosrowshahi, the 'new' CEO of Uber. Not only because of who he is as a person but also to be able to get insights into the company and see if and how he's cleaning house after all the scandals.

Which article or video do you recommend to your customers?

Helping our clients to build new digital ventures, there is nothing more important than fending off day two. Here is part of a letter from Jeff Bezos to the Amazon shareholders that explains this more: "Day Two is stasis. Followed by irrelevance. Followed by excruciating, painful decline. Followed by death. To be sure, this kind of decline would happen in extreme slow motion. An established company might harvest Day Two for decades, but the final results would still come." In my opinion the entire letter is a must-read for entrepreneurs and any established company in the world.

Tell us something about your personal life. What do you do in your free time, if there is any?
Some time ago, a business partner of mine said, "Your life is like a hot plate with four fields. One field is your family, the second is your job, the third is friends and the fourth is hobbies and sports. Unfortunately, you'll only manage to deal with three of the four plates at a time." My fourth plate is sports. I would love to have more time to go running, play squash, tennis or go snowboarding in the mountains.

What do you like most about working in Frankfurt? What's so special about the city?
Frankfurt and the Rhine-Main area is where I was born and grew up, so for me there's kind of a natural connection to the region. For me, it's not just about Frankfurt, but it's about whatever you can see and do within a few minutes of travelling around; for instance, going downhill biking at the Feldberg. Frankfurt is also my window to the world, thanks to the international airport, which is again just a few minutes away from downtown. I had the chance to travel quite a lot in my business life, being able to gain work experience in Barcelona and San Francisco, but coming back to Frankfurt always meant coming home for me.

There are just a few things that bother me a bit about Frankfurt. One of these is the low availability of funds for startups. Frankfurt is known as the city of finance and banking, with multiple companies from the industry who have their headquarters here. It might imply that there should be sufficient funds for startups available, but what we see is the opposite. The ecosystem needs to enable these players. When it comes to Series A or B funding, the list of investors usually doesn't have anyone from Frankfurt on it. Lucky for us, Frankfurt is developing in this area – slowly but steadily.

[About]   Candylabs enables corporations and SMEs to develop and implement new digital ventures and innovative products. With customers in HR, insurance, real estate, finance, banking, chemistry and pharmaceuticals, Candylabs has already established new digital ventures and successfully brought new digital product offerings to the market.

[Links]   Web: **candylabs.de** Facebook: **candylabsHQ** Twitter: **@candylabsHQ**

What are your top work essentials?
Laptop and my small old-school offline notebook.

At what age did you found your company?
Twenty-seven. However, I had my first side
business when I was twenty-one.

What's your most-used app?
Probably Slack.

**What's the most valuable piece of advice
you've been given?**
It's rather important to have the right peers
for the right questions.

What's your greatest skill?
I am often valued as the most ambitious.
That helps in certain areas, but not in all areas.

Eric-Jan Krausch

Founder and CEO / Acomodeo

Eric-Jan Krausch, the forward-thinking and flip-flop-wearing founder and CEO of Acomodeo, first came up with the idea for the serviced-apartment platform with his former flatmate David Wohde. Prior to founding Acomodeo, Eric-Jan worked as a strategic and creative marketing consultant, specializing in eye-tracking technology for product design and usability research. This was a natural follow-up to receiving an MA in Digital Pioneering from Friedrichshafen/Cambridge and a BA in Music Business from Mannheim. With a varied innovation background, Eric-Jan is passionate about coming up with creative solutions and empowering young professionals, and he has a style and sense of humor all his own.

What does your company do, and how is it unique in the housing market?
We are like Airbnb but for business, in that we are brokering serviced apartments. That's one of the major USPs where we are different than Airbnb and vacation rentals. We have a worldwide supply, we aggregate it, we enrich it, and we make it directly bookable. We're not brokering shared properties or private inventory. This has given us a worldwide customer base of corporate customers – 95 percent of our customers are corporate – who are dedicated to this special product. So the fit is very nice because our supply is able to provide long stays in a professional environment with all kinds of services that you know from hotels but with more space than the classical hotel room, perfect for expatriates looking to relocate on project business.

How did you originally come up with the idea for Acomodeo?
In 2013, I was living in a shared flat with David. He had an agency for brokering apartments, manually doing apartment bookings for big events. The business model was more based on having a clear inventory, a huge number of people booking, and brokering different kinds of things. At this time, I was working in an agency and consulted a marketplace for classic cars. I saw the problems that David and his agency was facing, and one of them was related to the peak booking times for events. Like, with the World Cup, you only get those events every four years. In the meantime, the customers were requesting apartments for single trips. And it wasn't really economical to do these bookings because the search was taking too long, negotiation was taking too long, and payment is not very standardized in the market. So we totally saw the gap that we wanted to close, between business travelers and professional supply.

Can you tell us more about the beginning stages of Acomodeo?

When we started in 2015, the mission statement was we wanted to make booking a serviced apartment as easy as booking a hotel, and we thought there would be hotel infrastructure we could easily reuse. We couldn't have known then how outdated tourism IT tends to be. So one of the first steps was actually to bring in a state-of-the-art infrastructure. So we had multi-currencies, we had different kinds of standardization – all that had to be consolidated and standardized in our own ecosystem. That's what we call the Acomodeo ecosystem: one environment capable of doing these bookings on its own. We're one of the first to have average length of stays of eighty-seven nights or booking for two years of accommodation in one single booking in the corporate environment. This is a totally different market, so we created a system which fits perfectly into these processes and is reliable. If you want to get into big corporations, they have to trust you. I bet every startup faces these troubles when it comes to reaching big customers. It's a hell of a ride.

Sounds like it! How did it develop from there?

You can see every day that people want things to be easy. That's why the impact of Airbnb is so huge on the hospitality market and why we wanted to launch Acomodeo. It took us around a year and a half to find people who'd invest in this idea, because everybody was afraid of the amount of money you need to create the basic infrastructure to have the ability to do proper B2B sales. In March 2015 we found investors, and this was the kickoff. It took us around one and a half years to build an automated process and system that was ready for sales. That was the point where we said, "BAM! Now we're going," with bigger clients, big group bookings for car manufacturers, and some complete relocations for musical casts and crews. We enriched our ecosystem with different kinds of software solutions to manage inventory, and we even created a fully customizable white-label version for corporates, which launched in November 2017.

Can you tell us about mistakes that have defined the Acomodeo journey?

One of the biggest mistakes was not focusing enough on the management structure of the company. It's normal for every kind of company, especially if you have a B2B business, to need people that have experience, with a structure where everyone can play to their strengths. You need to separate performers from non-performers so that you don't have people of similar personalities too close together, not seeing the problems you'd identify if you had a better structure in place. Also, we are a very, very young team, with an average age of twenty-eight to twenty-nine, which can be very challenging.

"*I want everyone to feel secure enough to ask 'the stupid questions,' because often some people see things that others missed for years.*"

Can you elaborate on building a business with a young staff?

Dealing with a young staff can be at times challenging yet extremely rewarding. Of course, young professionals who have been in the workforce for just a few years require more training time and are bound to make mistakes, but even senior level talents in major companies make mistakes. A young staff is more willing to admit they made a mistake or that they need advice on how to complete a certain task. They perceive this as part of their learning process, which indeed it is. When you reach a certain senior level, sometimes you have the feeling you need to maintain a particular "expert" status, which in a way limits you and makes you more reluctant to admit that some processes you're used to can be changed and improved. In this sense, having a relatively young staff is rewarding, as people don't have a mental blockage of how things have to be done. They don't follow the usual linear processes; instead, they're creating their own. The benefit of working with young professionals and even a young team is that statements like "we've always done it that way" don't occur, or let's say only occur rarely.

Can you identify the best decision you ever made for Acomodeo?

The best decision was to hire people that didn't have any clue about tourism. This helped us to create an infrastructure and to continuously work on this system so that it fit to our needs. Our whole development team does not come from a travel-experience background, so every time we're facing problems, we don't think in the classical "it can't be done" mentality you'd have if you'd already worked with all the travel solutions in the market. It was a different kind of approach that no one was thinking about: all about having out-of-the-box creative magic. It was by far the most fascinating way to show corporates the way it could, and actually does, work.

What has been your experience founding in Frankfurt? And what is the ecosystem like?

Founding Acomodeo in Frankfurt has been great for our purposes. Within the Rhine-Main region, there's a large number of corporates and financial companies as well as consultancy companies, which opened up great opportunities for us and gave us the B2B focus of our solutions. I don't think we could have chosen a better place. Moreover, Frankfurt is an extremely international and vibrant city, and this has helped us grow our company with talent from all over the world and the chance to create valuable connections globally.

Based on your experience now, can you share some advice with other younger startups?
Founding is not only the idea and the business plan; it's more the execution. To take the time
to be able to do this properly, to solve all kinds of problems you have in your company,
especially communications, is the biggest thing. How to structure communication, how to
structure distribution of information, how to make sure information is not lost. The most
important part of all this is to be authentic. I'm always playing on the fact that I'm twenty-
eight-years young, especially when the rest of the room is thinking, "What is this child telling
me?" At the end people see when you're not authentic, so it is important to have layers of
communication between professional and personal.

Can you speak more about authentic communication in your role as CEO?
Within Acomodeo, we strive to have a constant two-way communication stream, meaning that
everyone is encouraged and welcomed to share opinions regardless of their level of expertise.
Brilliant ideas come from various places. As the CEO, I make sure that each "Acomodian,"
meaning Acomodeo employee, has the freedom to explore and give new ideas, regardless
of how crazy they might sound. I want everyone to feel secure enough to ask "the stupid
questions," because often some people see things that others missed for years. Of course,
not all ideas are great, and this is where authentic communication comes in handy. I can
assure employees that their ideas will be heard and that they can expect honest, genuine
feedback in return. Open, authentic communication benefits us on many levels – motivational,
organizational, you name it. I always aim to communicate in this way, which enables the heads
of our departments to do the same, and so on.

[About]   Acomodeo is a unique hotel-booking platform that connects long-stay accommodation
with the worldwide travel market, specializing in serviced apartments. Founded in 2015,
the company aggregates over 400,000 properties in 120 counties and strives to be the most
streamlined technical solution for companies looking to find homes wherever their business
takes them.

[Links]   Web: **acomodeo.com** Facebook: **acomodeo** Instagram: **acomodeo**

What are your top work essentials?
My calendar, good structure, and a clean head.

At what age did you found your company?
Twenty-five.

What's your most-used app?
Slack, Gmail, DeepL, Salesforce.

**What's the most valuable piece of advice
you've been given?**
Ask people for advice. If you don't ask, you stay stupid.

What's your greatest skill?
I come up with creative, executable solutions.

Jana Ehret

Founder / CoWorkPlay

Jana Ehret is the founder of CoWorkPlay in Frankfurt. She's a trend expert and futurologist with a degree in cultural anthropology and literature. She was working in marketing and communications at black chili when she founded CoWorkPlay in 2016.

How did you fall into entrepreneurship?
My parents came to Germany from Russia in 1991, and both of them are entrepreneurs. I have it in my blood. My dad had a lot of different ideas – he was always like a big child – and my mom as well. They have their own company, and now their daughter is also an entrepreneur. I came to Frankfurt eleven years ago from Bremen to study. Starting with law, I switched to literature after five semesters when I realized that law wasn't something I wanted to do. I finished my studies in literature, and my parents asked me, "Where are you going, and what will you do in your life?" I told them I didn't know yet, but that I'd find a way.

During my studies, I was working in theater and in restaurant and catering jobs on the side. Here is where I figured out that I needed to do something where I could get in touch with people on a daily basis, help people and build a network.

When I was twenty-eight, I had the same questions from my parents as when I was eighteen, but I also had "When will you be a mother?" I told them, "Don't worry; children will come." I was on holidays in Vietnam, sitting at a bungalow in the sun and deciding what to do with my life. I asked myself, "Should I study and get a master's, or get a job or start a family?" That's where CoWorkPlay came from. I didn't want to have to choose one or the other. I wanted a job where I could continue to learn and also be a mother at the same time.

What does CoWorkPlay do?
We are the very first family-friendly coworking space in Frankfurt. We have a special place for children between the ages of six months and three years. Their parents can work here just like a normal coworking space, and there are "flying nannies" who take care of the children. The uniqueness here is that CoWorkPlay is not just for parents. We are for children, for parents and for professionals who are not parents as well. We have this unique connection for everyone. In addition to this, we have a big event space for external and internal events. It's all about the members getting in touch with each other and fulfilling their purposes in life.

I had the idea for this coworking space in 2016, and we founded CoWorkPlay at the end of the year. I started the company with a friend of mine using the business model canvas in my working room. My background really has nothing to do with business. My background is creative; I'm a writer and a painter. The whole modus operandi behind CoWorkPlay was to think big. I wanted a place to host all of the activities I was planning to do. After not even a year, my business partner left, so I made a post on a well-known Facebook group. It said that a young founder is looking for a partner, and black chili came up as a player. At black chili, I met Yvonne. She became the second cofounder of CoWorkPlay. Together, we started working on the business very intensively. We soft-launched the space in December 2016, and we had the official opening in January 2017. In August 2018, we opened the second floor at the Eastside location. In October 2018, we opened our second space at a famous Frankfurt shopping mall, MyZeil.

What is black chili?

Many people asked us if we were going to get an investor to support CoWorkPlay financially. In the end, we decided to go with black chili, a company builder, and they filled the holes we had in our business. Yvonne was good at law and HR, I am creative, and black chili had the all-round support we needed. They helped everywhere and answered my questions. Of course, I also went to different events in order to learn as much as I could about running a business.

In the beginning, I had many questions. Some of the common ones were what is the right form you should use to found the company, or what are the most important things you should think about when signing a contract for a location? Black chili had the answers we needed. They also have a lot of experience in marketing and sales – basically everything you need as a founder. I worked for black chili for about a year, and Yvonne still works for them. Now I'm with CoWorkPlay full time.

What was one of your early challenges when starting up? And how did you overcome it?

We had a lot of problems when starting out. It was two years before we were able to successfully found CoWorkPlay. There were a lot of problems we had in regards to time. What I mean by this is that it took a very long time to find a space for CoWorkPlay. Many landlords didn't know or didn't fully understand what coworking really meant, and when we started, WeWork wasn't in Frankfurt yet. Since WeWork entered the Frankfurt market, landlords now say, "Okay, we know a bit about coworking." Before, no one could understand it. And then, when you combined coworking with children, absolutely no one could understand this. Then there were the credit checks, which took about two months. These were the two biggest difficulties in the beginning.

« *We have a wonderful culture where failure isn't failure anymore, and even if you do fail, you will learn a lot.* »

We signed the contract for our space at the beginning of November and moved in at the end of December. We had a small budget, because we initially planned for a much smaller space than we ended up with. We had planned for 800 square meters but ended up having a 1,200 square meter space, so we had to think about how to create a wonderful, creative space without spending too much money. We had a lot of help from our families and friends to find the right furniture and decorate the space.

In the beginning, I was very blue-eyed and thought that I would open the doors to CoWorkPlay and everyone would show up. It took some time for us to become known and established in the Rhine-Main region. Getting people to think of CoWorkPlay when they thought about coworking took time. Lots of people also thought they had to be parents to work in our space, but that's absolutely not true. We're open for parents but also for people who don't have children.

What was one of your best decisions?

One of my best decisions ever was founding CoWorkPlay. It was everything I ever wanted to do. In August, we had the *Gründerbericht*, something like a founder's report in English. Yvonne and I were doing a recap of the past two years and realized that founding the company was the best decision. During the entire process of starting up, there were lots of highs and lows, but our partners were always behind us to support us on this journey. I would do it again in an instant. I can't imagine not being a founder!

If you could go back in time and do something differently, what would it be?

If I could go back in time, I would feel more comfortable in the founder role. For example, my first business partner was a man, and when we'd go for location visits, the building managers and landlords would only speak to him. I would think to myself, "Okay, but I'm the founder!"

I think I'd also be a bit pushier and more confident. I'd definitely say to past Jana, "Be more self-confident, because what you're doing is great! Many people love it. Don't be shy, don't be afraid; everything always turns into something good." And I'd also try to get the right partners on board from the beginning.

What is one piece of professional advice you'd give to people who are just starting out?

Don't be afraid, and just do it. Just jump. Even as cold as the water is, just do it. You can't do anything wrong, because in today's society it's totally okay to fail. We have a wonderful culture where failure isn't failure anymore, and even if you do fail, you will learn a lot. Even if CoWorkPlay didn't work, it would still be the best thing I have done in my life.

What do you like about working in Frankfurt?

It's so multicultural. I grew up next to Bremen, and I was the only one from a Russian family in this very German city. When I came to Frankfurt, there were so many cultures and people from all nationalities, and everyone was so open minded! I love this. From the founder's perspective, Frankfurt has a lot more to offer than just fintech. It's very colorful and lively. It's difficult, yes, because you don't have the same entrepreneurial spirit as in Berlin, but it's definitely on its way to getting there.

[About]   CoWorkPlay is a modern and familiar coworking space in Frankfurt. From shared desks and offices to event and meeting spaces, they offer everything you need as a freelancer, corporate or startup. Daycare for children and postnatal care are available onsite, as well as everything else a regular coworking space offers.

What are your top work essentials?
My laptop and a very cozy space where to work.

At what age did you found your company?
Twenty-nine.

What's your most-used app?
Slack is one of the best things ever. Pipedrive
and LexOffice are amazing.

**What's the most valuable piece of advice
you've been given?**
When other people say you think too big,
tell them they think too small.

What's your greatest skill?
Having the creativity and imagination
to see things that are not yet here.

Mario Hachemer

CTO / FastBill

Mario Hachemer has been active in the Frankfurt startup scene since 2011 and created the first Startup Weekend in Frankfurt in 2012. It was at this event he met the CEO of FastBill and joined the FastBill team as CTO in 2015. He's also the founder of Gründerstammtisch, a monthly meetup for early-stage founders in Frankfurt.

How did you get involved in technology and startups?
I started programming at the age of twelve or thirteen, and I found myself working in IT companies at around sixteen. After working for a couple of years in tech, it was a surprise that most entrepreneurs were failing at tech, because this was never my problem. I was always able to help lots of people, doing intros to programmers or other tech workers. This is probably why many people often refer to me when they have a problem with their business.

What is Gründerstammtisch?
The Gründerstammtisch, or "Founders' Table" in English, is the largest meetup of its kind in Frankfurt. They are mostly people who are almost founders: people who are thinking about becoming founders but are on the fence. I try to kick people off the fence. You only live once; you might as well become an entrepreneur.

Recently, a fourteen year-old boy asked me if he could attend the Founders' Table. He asked if he could speak with others about entrepreneurship, because it's hard for him to talk about wanting to start a business with his classmates – nobody in his school is interested in it. I could relate deeply with this, so I invited him over and asked if he could bring a parent with him. His mother joined, and I got the chance to meet a real hero that day. Seeing her being supportive of her son's aspirations – whatever they may be – to such a degree was inspiring.

In essence, that's what Founders' Table is about. It is a melting pot of people who want to talk about entrepreneurship. We try not to have someone, for example, a VC, sponsor the event, so that people can speak honestly and freely about their issues. When people get up and say, for example, "My husband wants to leave me because I work on my startup so much," or, "I missed my son's game because of my startup," that's not something you feel safe talking about in the vicinity of investors or other potential partners or customers. But these are experiences many entrepreneurs share.

I try to be a little bit like the barkeeper of the region and tend to keep everyone's misery close to me. It really helps when you want to do community building. I knew I had something precious with these one hundred and fifty people that attended the first Startup Weekend, and I just had to spend time fostering relationships with them.

How does a typical Founders' Table run?

We start around seven in the evening, and the official program starts at eight. There's always a short introduction, then the official program, then networking. This is when I tell people to try and talk about their specialty. For example, "I'm the electrical engineering gal," or, "I'm the online marketing guy." This way, other people can remember you and talk about things you have in common, or they might even partner with you.

Every two to three months, we have a pitch round with three to four pitches. These ideas are usually works in progress. After the pitch, the founders will receive valuable feedback. Then there is beer. The atmosphere is extremely vibrant. People are always commenting on the great people they meet. Most of the stuff I don't even hear because I can't see it from all angles all of the time. After the official program is over, people go to bars together. It's been like this since 2012, and it happened right after the first Startup Weekend began.

How were you involved in Startup Weekend?

I was working on startup ideas in 2009. I worked for months on projects without seeing any valuable outcome. I developed games, an affiliate marketing page and a tool for fundraising. All of those projects failed because I was the one-man army behind all of them, doing everything from all aspects of programming to marketing to finance, and I was only proficient enough in the tech space back then. In mid 2010, I got very depressed, because nothing seemed to pan out, and at my university back then I didn't find any support or interest from other students. A friend from Munich told me about a Startup Weekend in Amsterdam, to which we went on the wild guess that it would at least be a cool experience. What I found there was the kind of community I knew I needed.

With the experience gathered from organizing events in the tech space previously, I got the confidence to do something similar in Frankfurt. I found the first sponsors for Startup Weekend in Frankfurt in 2012. Two companies that were founded at this event are still around, and one of them now has twenty-five employees. We did two more Startup Weekends in 2014 and 2015. After that, I wanted to join FastBill to focus on solving the bureaucracy nightmare that is entrepreneurship in Germany. In addition, I became a dad in 2016. This is why it's been a long three years since the last Startup Weekend. I approached a few people to take over the organizer position, but it hasn't worked out yet.

" I knew I had something precious with these one hundred and fifty people that attended the first Startup Weekend, and I just had to spend time fostering relationships with them. "

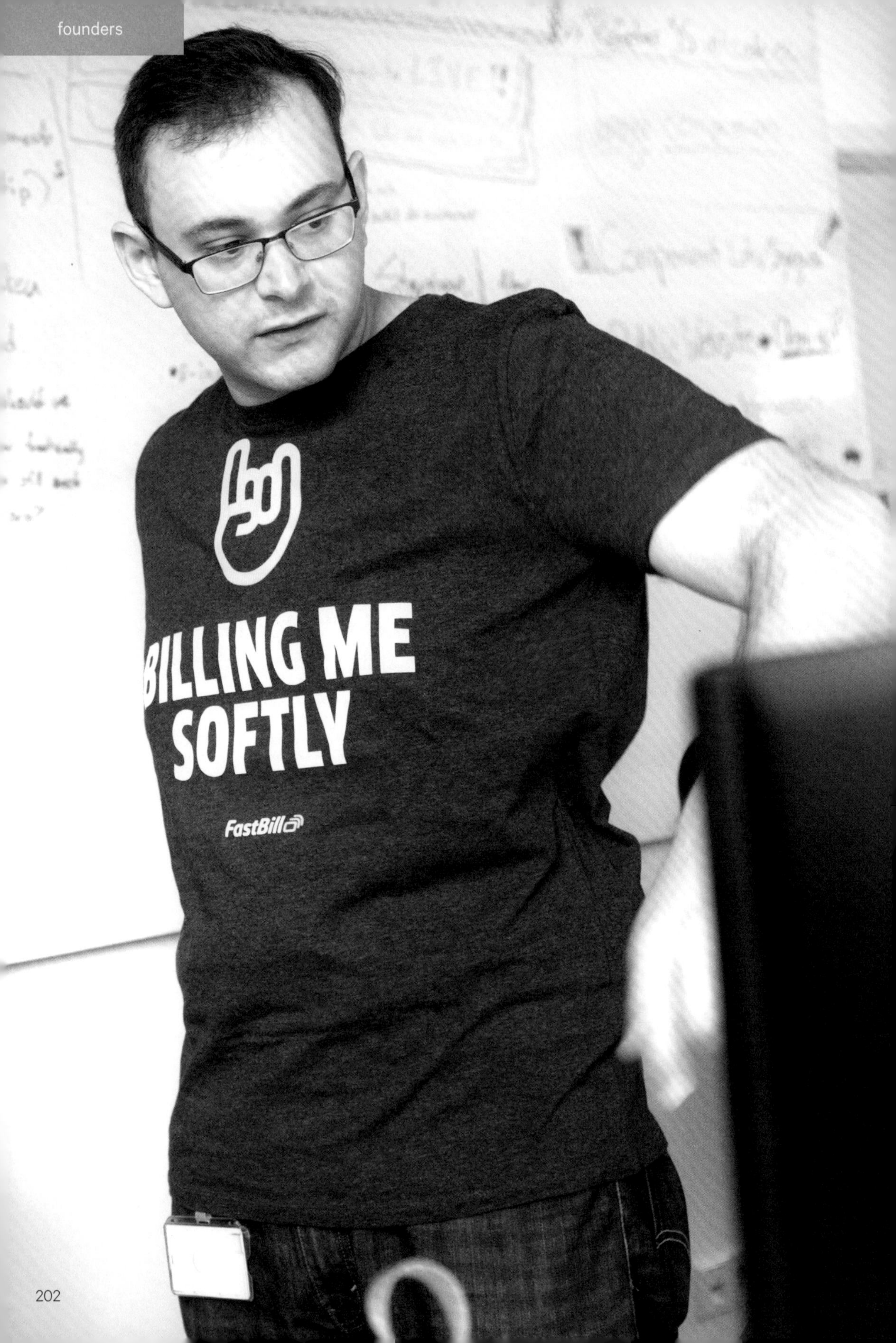
BILLING ME
SOFTLY
FastBill

When we organized Startup Weekend, the community got a lot of energy out of it, and more startups grew out of that. I always wanted to be in the presence of people who want to do things. In Frankfurt, it's relatively easy to get a good-paying job, but having the courage to start something on your own is rare. If you meet someone here who goes out and doesn't stop after eight weeks, it's something very special. In my experience, these people also often make great friends.

Why is eight weeks a turning point for startups?
The first eight weeks, I would say, are very euphoric. People are very enthusiastic. You start talking to other people about your idea. That can be a big step. Even getting negative feedback and criticism is a driver. Founders will think, "I'll prove them wrong." This goes away after five weeks because you have to pay your bills. This also affects younger founders more than older founders, because they're a bit more optimistic.

The next step is getting other people to believe in the idea. Not finding their first cofounder or employee is the make-or-break point, because there is no one-man founding-army. Even Elon Musk has lots of people working closely with him. You certainly don't get that as a new founder. The next thing is being able to structure their finances. In my experience, most founders run into debt after the second four weeks. Then they get scared that they can't get their finances in order, and they can't get other people to believe in their idea. They say, "I'll go get a job until my idea gets fleshed out," and never work on it again.

This is the value of Startup Weekend, I believe. You kind of get to learn the importance of convincing other people at the same time as treating your resources and time as precious. You have these eight weeks condensed into three days. But, of course, nothing is like the real thing.

How did you meet the founder of FastBill?
Every Startup Weekend needs a jury. Most of my network at that time was software developers, so I asked if anyone knew really amazing founders. Some people said, "You have to check out Offenbach", which some say is the Bronx of Frankfurt. "You have to go there and talk to René; he's building a SaaS accounting thing." So I went and had coffee with him at his office, and he said he wanted to be part of the jury. He did a great job on the jury, giving very convertible advice to our participants. We kept in touch for three years, from 2012 to 2015. I'd taken over an agency, and I didn't want to do consulting work anymore by that time. At the end of 2015, we decided to merge the two companies together, and I became the CTO of FastBill, with all of our employees getting respective roles as well.

What do you like about working in Frankfurt?

When I work in Frankfurt, I feel at the center of things. There's still lots of stuff to do here, but the general vibe is a lot more concentrated on work than in Berlin. It's also the smallest metropolitan city in the world. You can cross the city by bike in an hour, but there are skyscrapers and a massive airport. You have the best of both worlds. If I had to describe Frankfurt in a few words, I'd say it's healthy at everything. It's not the most picturesque place in the world, but it is really beautiful. It's not the most exciting city in any specific category, but there is always opportunity to party, make friends and do world-changing business around every corner. It's not a small, safe town, but it's still a great place to raise your kids and expose them to a world of experiences. You don't have to make many compromises here, from my point of view. I can do everything I want here, although I may not get the newest hipster donut the week it's available in New York or San Francisco. That's still a great deal for me.

[About]   FastBill provides simplified, smart and beautiful accounting solutions for small and medium businesses. Customers can automate daily operations and bring order to their invoices, receipts and banking.

[Links]   Web: fastbill.com Facebook: fastbillnews Twitter: @fastbillnews

What are your top work essentials?
My smartphone and laptop.

At what age did you found your company?
Founders' Table and Startup Weekend at twenty-four.

What's your most-used app?
Slack, definitely.

**What's the most valuable piece of advice
you've been given?**
If you're annoyed at something, don't make people
around you annoyed. René at FastBill taught me this.

What's your greatest skill?
Knowing people, what they're good at, and making
the right connections at the right time.

Vishal Rai

Cofounder and CEO / Acellere

Vishal Rai is an entrepreneur with a passion for software engineering. Originally from India, he has lived and worked all over the world and has a keen insight into both the cultural impact of startups and trends in the global ecosystem. Vishal was an engineer with a background in telecommunications before founding Acellere in 2009. He describes himself as having been naively optimistic at the start of his entrepreneurial career. At present, he is a battle-hardened innovator with an endless capacity to wax lyrical about startups, technology and the future.

How did you end up as an entrepreneur in Frankfurt?

It was pure destiny. I was working for a very large company in Seattle. I had the opportunity at a very young age to come to Europe by my previous employer to lead a division in Continental Europe. I was in my twenties and had never been to Europe, so I came. I was with this company originally in India, then in the US, then through them, I came here and grew the business in Europe. As a part of this journey, I saw the opportunity that would become what my company is all about today. This was 2009. There was blood on the streets, the Lehmann crash had happened, everyone was running for the hills. However, as someone wise once said, "Never waste a good crisis to start something new." That's when everything is really affordable. And that's what I did. I saw the opportunity.

How did you come up with the idea for Acellere and Gamma?

I saw very early on that software was going to be ubiquitous and in our bodies, and I was very nervous with the way software was being developed across the planet. With software pervading every part of our lives, if this was the quality of software that was being developed, it could lead to cataclysmic consequences. So software, good software, has to be taken seriously. Software should be built like we build planes and bridges today. It should never fail – failure should have negative consequences. Software runs our world; therefore, we have to build software with a bit more precision. The quality of engineers hasn't kept up in scale. Good engineers are either expensive or rare. Compared to the demand for experienced software engineers in the industry, the supply just isn't there. This leads to a war for good talent in the industry, and either firms pay exorbitant amounts for experienced software engineers or have to make do with the less experienced ones. So what do you do? The way to solve this is not by increasing salaries and hiring people, because you don't have the people in numbers; the way you do it is you build machines to augment human capabilities so that engineers can still write software with precision and with quality, without the engineer limitations I mentioned.

That's the opportunity I saw way back in 2009. Bear in mind that in 2009, very few had confidence in artificial intelligence or awareness about it, and that's when my cofounder and I said, "Let's build a platform that helps people write better software using machine learning." We were perhaps one of the first platforms of its kind, applying artificial intelligence in software engineering.

Can you expand a bit more on how software will be in our bodies?

We already have people in the Nordics who have chip implants that they use for cool applications. These implants essentially work by writing software onto these chips. Without software, these chips are useless foreign bodies. In the coming days when we start having more such devices in our bodies, they'll have millions of lines of code running helping them do their functions. Now imagine if that software was poorly designed: the consequences could be fatal. That's why we should take software design very seriously now.

In basic terms, how does the Gamma platform work?

Gamma's core mission is to help people write better software, faster. We've developed our own algorithms based on the first principles of software engineering. When you scan your software through our platform, Gamma, it'll find the structural issues in the software and tell you how you can go about fixing them. Additionally, it will show you if one component is connected to another component that has a structural anomaly, which is very important in understanding the impact of structural anomalies in code. We have a prioritization algorithm that does the thinking for you and helps our users focus on the biggest hotspots. And we haven't stopped at finding issues alone: we also have a recommendation engine that suggests how the identified hotspots can be fixed. If you use open source, you can sign up for Gamma online and use it for free.

What were some early struggles, and how did you overcome them?

Initially, it was really difficult to convince investors in Germany to put money into the business. Now things have changed dramatically, and the investors are much smarter. Back then, the investors were still very traditional and most of them were non-entrepreneurs. We must have met around forty investors within the first six months to no avail. It was very difficult. Then we decided that since we are already experienced people, we have the algorithms in our minds, so we'll look around and see if there are software projects that are in trouble and offer them our consulting services to help them overcome the challenges. Luckily for us, some of the biggest companies around us were having software disasters in their business. Big companies loved it! We would do audits, we would use our algorithms on those projects, and things worked very well. We actually built our software-analytics platform in conjunction with the realities of the industry, and hence our platform is very effective and actually works as it's meant to.

" Running and building a company is bloody hard. A sane person would actually quit. You have to have passion. Insanity and passion are two sides of the same coin."

Vishal Rai

What do you think was your biggest mistake, and your best decision, in creating Acellere?
I think the biggest mistake I made was that I underestimated the effort I needed to evaluate
people when I was building my team. When you're building a team and you're a young
company, you hire people who may be very good in a role – let's say, a project manager – but
who may not be the right folks as entrepreneurs. So choose your team wisely. I'll say this to all
entrepreneurs, running and building a company is bloody hard. A sane person would actually
quit. You have to have passion. Insanity and passion are two sides of the same coin.

Are there things you learned along the way you could use as advice for other startups?
It's something so obvious right? I'll take the example of the iPhone. There were smartphones
before, like from Nokia and Ericsson. People assumed Nokia was the future of smartphones,
until Steve came and proved them wrong. Apple didn't invent the smartphone; they just
innovated the hell out of it, and the rest, as they say, is history. That's how true innovations have
always been – always better than invention. Similarly, Google wasn't the first search engine,
but what Larry and Sergey did is made a search engine that was insanely simple to use, just like
the iPhone. What pioneers like Apple and Google did is they just made their technology easy
to use. We often underestimate the person using the tech today and have this bad habit of
over-engineering products and losing out on the actual use of the same. We in Acellere have
been inspired by all the above and are aiming to do the same with our platform.

**How do you define great product design and technology, and how does Acellere
address that?**
Bad design leads to poor quality products. That holds true for software as well. Since we didn't
find any platforms in the market that identified that in software, we decided to make one
ourselves. These were the founding principles of our platform.

**Can you expand on what makes beautiful software, and what design principles you may
have taken from other industries to implement in software design?**
A well-designed software is one that is designed well from the inside. It's structurally cohesive,
the code is clean, the logic is efficient and the overheads are minimal. An example of bad
structural design is a God Class. A class is a base unit in software, and a God Class is one that
does too many things that are not cohesive. As an example, imagine if we had one person on
a football team who was responsible for defending, attacking and goalkeeping. What could
happen to that individual if he got injured? The team would not perform well. That's exactly
how well-designed software should be written: components should have clear responsibilities.
The worrying part is that developers sometimes can't see how well the components they write
are designed and hence are unaware of the consequences. With Gamma, we can surface these
design anomalies and help users identify and fix them.

What was your experience starting up a company in the Frankfurt ecosystem?
Frankfurt is a very underestimated city. I think it's one of the most vibrant cities I've ever lived in. The multi-ethnicity of the people here makes the city very welcoming, especially as a foreigner. It may not be as big as Paris or San Francisco in size, but in some ways it feels like a big city. You also get a lot of local networks that really love and support entrepreneurs. Many locals have an international footprint, and they're ambitious and educated. They want to break the mold of Frankfurt being a banking city alone. And you almost know everyone here, so it's easy to expand your network as a startup.

[About]   Acellere is the maker of Gamma, an intelligent software analytics platform that finds structural problems in code, identifies the most pressing issues, prioritizes them, and assists developers in fixing the problems, all powered by advanced software-engineering algorithms and applied machine-learning and artificial-intelligence technology.

What are your top work essentials?
Thinking space and thinking time. And my phone.

At what age did you found your company?
Thirties.

What's your most-used app?
Headspace, Spotify, and Mail.

**What's the most valuable piece of advice
you've been given?**
Overnight success is going to be ten years, so dig
in for the long haul.

What's your greatest skill?
Perseverance, flexibility, and gut instinct in building teams.

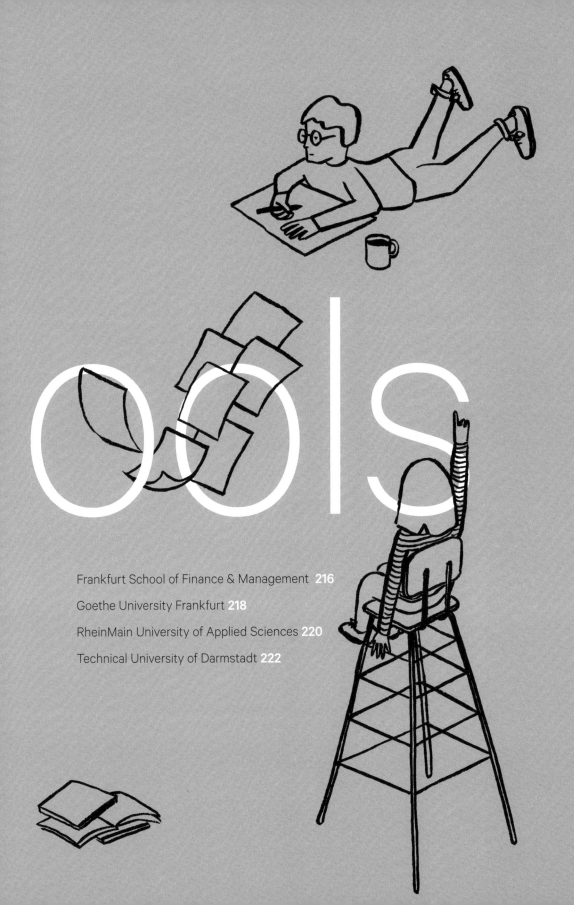

ools

- **Be authentic.**
  We're looking for individuals who will add diversity and drive to our international program and who will develop and learn from others.

- **Have a plan for the future.**
  Tell us how studying at Frankfurt School will help you become the entrepreneur you want to be in the future.

- **Share your entrepreneurial ideas.**
  Don't be shy; include your business ideas in your application. We're interested in many aspects beyond your grades in the application.

- **Share your personal experience.**
  Strong grades are an excellent start, but we're also looking for life experience. Internships and international experience are looked at positively in your application.

- **Join us at an event.**
  Meet us in person before starting to get some insights about what makes a great application from the people who will be looking it over.

[Name]

Frankfurt School of Finance & Management

[Elevator Pitch]

"We are a business school with an entrepreneurial mindset. We also provide access to finance for aspiring founders, and academic research opportunities in areas such as blockchain, AI and fintech."

[Enrollment]

2,370 (2018)

[Description]

Founded in 1957 as an initiative for training banking professionals, Frankfurt School of Finance & Management is one of the leading business schools in Europe. Entrepreneurship is integrated into each and every program, and entrepreneurs can hone their management skills with executive education programs. In addition, the Triple Crown-accredited business school provides conferences, guest lectures, meetups and its own Startup Night. Tuition fees per semester start at €7,000, but there are a variety of scholarships available to students. "At the Frankfurt School, the future entrepreneur will not only gain skills and tools but also develop connections to investors, receive advice on financial aspects, and benefit from an international alumni network," says Prof. Dr. Nils Stieglitz, president at Frankfurt School of Finance & Management.

Prospective students can participate in one of the school's recruitment events to meet and greet the faculty and staff before applying online. All bachelor-degree students complete a hands-on course called How to Build a Startup. Students are coached by successful entrepreneurs and develop a viable business in six weeks. The Master and MBA programs offer both modules and degree concentrations on international entrepreneurship, digital business and entrepreneurial management. Some of the courses offered include Managing the Growing Entrepreneurial Venture and Social Entrepreneurship and Impact Investing. MBA students also have the option to develop a business plan as their final thesis.

There are a number of on-campus centers which explore the impact of technology on business. The Frankfurt School Blockchain Center is a think tank and research center investigating the implications of blockchain technology on companies and their business models. The Centre for Human and Machine Intelligence conducts basic and applied research at the intersection of artificial intelligence and machine learning, social and decision science, and finance and management. Between fifty and sixty startups have emerged from Frankfurt School in a variety of sectors since 2015.

[Apply to]

frankfurt-school.de

[Links]

Web: **frankfurt-school.de** Facebook: **FrankfurtSchool** Twitter: **@FrankfurtSchool**

- **Do your research.**
  With over 140 undergraduate programs and 70
  masters programs to choose from, each with different
  entry requirements, you should be sure to do your
  own research before applying.

- **Be autonomous.**
  Studying at Goethe University Frankfurt means
  that you should be self-driven and motivated during
  your studies.

- **Have a good level of German.**
  Though some courses are taught in English
  and German, a solid understanding of German
  can always help.

- **Uphold intellectual integrity.**
  The faculty are some of the best in the world, with
  high teaching and research standards, and they
  are looking for students who want to do fantastic
  academic work.

- **Be curious.**
  Some of the best alumni of the university have seen
  the world in new ways, and we want our students
  to explore the world by harnessing their curiosity.

[Name]

Goethe University Frankfurt

[Elevator Pitch]

"We're an internationally-recognized research university and the third-largest university in Germany, with a focus on providing the critical-thinking skills that students need for the twenty-first century."

[Enrollment]

48,075 (2018)

[Description]

Goethe University Frankfurt (Johann Wolfgang Goethe-Universität Frankfurt am Main) is the third-largest university in Germany by student enrollment and has five locations throughout the city. Founded in 1914 by the citizens of Frankfurt under the name Universität Frankfurt am Main, it was initially financed by wealthy families. Since its founding, there have been nineteen Nobel Prize winners who are alumni of the Goethe University Frankfurt. There are no tuition fees for undergraduate students, including international students, but there is a semester fee of around €350. Only master's degrees from the Goethe Business School, which are aimed at professionals with some work experience, are more expensive and cost between €21,000 and €35,000. In order for international students to receive a student visa, they must be able to show proof of funds to cover their first year's living costs equal to or exceeding €8,820.

The university has sixteen different faculties and offers both undergraduate and graduate degrees across the natural sciences, social sciences, law, philosophy, and business and economics. Students can apply online for both undergraduate and graduate programs with start dates in April and October.

For students interested in entrepreneurship, there is one elective course available per semester at the undergraduate and master's levels. The hands-on seminar-style course (with between fifteen and thirty students) is one of the last courses a student will take. "When I say it's hands on, we usually work with project partners who give us challenges," says Katharina Funke-Braun managing director of the Goethe Unibator, an incubator for innovation and entrepreneurship affiliated with the Goethe University Frankfurt. During the course, students learn to create and evaluate a solid business model by working with real-world problems presented by companies or entrepreneurs. "What we definitely see is that the awareness for the topic of entrepreneurship itself and for the startup area is definitely getting bigger," says Katharina.

[Apply to]

uni-frankfurt.de, or for international students, uni-assist.de

[Links]

Web: **uni-frankfurt.de** Facebook: **goetheuni** Twitter: **@goetheuni**

- **Be curious.**
  Students should do as much as they can
  to broaden their horizons, including getting
  as much information from others as possible
  in their entrepreneurial journeys.

- **Get connected.**
  Starting a company, whether as a student or
  graduate, is not something you do alone. While
  starting up, you want to make strong, lasting
  connections to build a supportive team and network.

- **Make the most of student life.**
  You're only a student once, so enjoy the learning
  process and don't rush into business life just yet.
  Founding as a student is a great opportunity, though
  you shouldn't forget to take advantage of being
  a student.

- **Get started.**
  Having an idea is one thing, but acting on that idea
  is another, so try your idea out. Try out an internship,
  join a company or start your own!

[Name]

RheinMain University of Applied Sciences

[Elevator Pitch]

"We offer seminars, workshops, and projects to improve your core skills and also provide advice and information about starting your professional life or your own business."

[Enrollment]

13,730 (2018)

[Description]

Located in the heart of the Rhine-Main region and spread across four campuses and five faculties, the RheinMain University of Applied Sciences is an innovative research university offering over seventy bachelor's and master's programs. Students enrolled in the university can choose from over seventy-five study programs and get access to a number of opportunities to join the startup ecosystem. RheinMain and its programs provide not only the tools for entrepreneurship but also a powerful network connected to the surrounding area. "We raise awareness toward entrepreneurship," says Gudrun Bolduan, project manager of the university's Competence & Career Center (CCC).

The CCC, one of RheinMain's chief entrepreneurial programs, offers students support, seminars, workshops and projects to improve core skills while also providing students with valuable information about starting up companies. It's a member of the startup network in Wiesbaden and RheinMain, where the campuses are located, and it gives members advice and organizes many events. In addition, it offers two extensive courses in business planning where students learn the approaches and tools needed to found a successful business. Students are encouraged to apply to funding programs in the RheinMain area to help accelerate their ideas and businesses. Enrollment in CCC programs is free for all RheinMain students.

Future student entrepreneurs can also join the university's international leadership program, which unites students from different European universities for an intensive learning week in July. Service-learning programs and social projects are also available (some for credit, depending on the course) are also offered to kickstart personal development. The university instills entrepreneurship in many of its study programs, with some concentrations requiring language or CCC modules to round out the technical courses. There are always opportunities to network and grow your student business, all year round. "We are happy to support student entrepreneurs in developing their new and fresh ideas," says Gudrun.

[Apply to]

hs-rm.de/en

[Links]

Web: **hs.rm/de/en/** Facebook: **HSRheinMain**

- Have proficiency in the German language.
  Regardless of your nationality, we require prospective students to demonstrate that they have adequate German language skills.

- Ask yourself why?
  To make a solid start, you need to make sure you're clear on what your motivation is and what you believe in.

- Be clear on your goals.
  We at TUD offer very specialized learning paths, so we want you to ask yourself, do your strengths and interests match your chosen degree program?

- Be ready to optimize your processes.
  Only when everything functions smoothly can you concentrate on new goals.

- Be a knowledge and technology based start up.
  We are experts for knowledge- and technology-based startups and have the competencies to really help those in this area.

[Name]

Technical University of Darmstadt

[Elevator Pitch]

"Since its founding in 1877, the Technical University of Darmstadt has contributed to the solution of urgent questions of the future with pioneering achievements and outstanding research and teaching. We focus on selected, highly relevant problem areas, and technology is the focus of all disciplines."

[Enrollment]

25,800 (2018)

[Description]

The Technical University of Darmstadt (Technische Universität Darmstadt), more commonly known as TU Darmstadt, is a research university on the outskirts of Frankfurt. Founded in 1877, it is one of Germany's leading technical universities (once recommended by Albert Einstein no less), and alumni include Nobel Laureates Prof. Dr. Peter Grünberg (Physics in 2007) and Prof. Dr. Ing. Gerhard Herzberg (Chemistry in 1971). TU Darmstadt is part of the TU9 alliance, a network of Germany's most prestigious and noteworthy universities of technology, and it has formed the strategic Rhine-Main Universities alliance alongside Goethe University Frankfurt and Johannes Gutenberg University Mainz.

TU Darmstadt has a wide range of disciplines, include engineering, mathematics, natural sciences and humanities, that revolve around the core of technology and provide the basis for more specific studies, such as research into IoT, digitalization, future energy systems, cybersecurity, matter and radiation science, and thermo-fluids and interfaces. The university's professors and students are dedicated to pursuing technologies and solutions via research to make a significant impact on the future.

TU Darmstadt has also created HIGHEST, their startup innovation branch with the aim of making startups in the fields of high-tech and digitization a success and creating strong entrepreneurship. HIGHEST is based on four pillars: Business Development/ Consultation, Teaching, Research/Innovation and Networking/Cooperation. Its startup consultants support TU Darmstadt students and scientists in making their ideas market-ready, and also supports experienced startups that want to grow and be adaptable to changing processes. TU Darmstadt and Highest also pursues what they call Vision 2020, in which all students at the university should have the opportunity to attend subjects from the fields of entrepreneurship, founding and innovation within their curriculum by the year 2020.

[Apply to]

master@pvw.tu-darmstadt.de

[Links]

Web: **tu-darmstadt.de** Facebook: **tudarmstadt** Twitter: **@TUDarmstadt**

stors

- **Have the right people.**
  We want to see a good combination of people for the
  team, with different strengths and skills but all "burning"
  for the same idea. Founding a company is not a sprint;
  it's a marathon.

- **Ask the right questions.**
  Is there really a need or problem for the solution you're
  working on? What about the market? Is it big enough
  and thus attractive for investors?

- **Spend time on your USPs.**
  Is the business idea really unique? Take a very close
  look at your competitors. Is there more than one USP to
  differentiate? Make sure your main USP meets the exact
  needs of your customers.

- **Remain flexible.**
  Adapt your business to the experiences you gain and
  to the feedback you get from your clients, mentors
  and investors. Try what works best for your business!

[Name]
Business Angels FrankfurtRheinMain e.V.

[Elevator Pitch]
"We're the largest business angel network in Germany. We support the startup ecosystem by performing workshops, events and awards. Our mission is to connect talented founders and innovative startups with business angels and venture capitalists."

[Sector]
All sectors

[Description]
Founded in 2000, Business Angels FrankfurtRheinMain is a registered nonprofit association with a long track record and a wide range of support to startups. It has a membership of more than 150 active business angels, including entrepreneurs and active or retired managers from various industries. Support can be given to startups not only in Frankfurt and Rhine-Main but also across all other German-speaking regions. There is no sector focus, which means any startup – from high-tech to no-tech – can apply. Individual or small groups of angels take only a minor stake, have a high commitment to the startups they invest in, and give smart money, which equates to funding, access to their professional network and general know-how.

"Approximately ten times a year, we have matching events with speed pitches for up to eight startups at an early stage," says board member Gabriele Acker-Bialek. "And twice a year, the more mature startups can take part in a Series A matching with VCs." Founders can also get personal feedback regarding their business plan and presentations at various startup events, or they can participate in a startup workshop to optimize their pitches to early-stage investors. Together with different partners, Business Angels FrankfurtRheinMain organizes the FinTechGermany Award for FinTech/InsurTech-Startups and for chemistry and similar sector startups, the ACHEMA-Gründerpreis.

Business Angels FrankfurtRheinMain wants to connect with founders and startups that have a profound business plan, a strong unique selling proposition and a high market potential. It's important to be "investment ready," meaning you should be well prepared, with a clear focus on target market, prototypes or a minimum viable product and, if applicable, patent applications and contacts to distribution partners and customers.

[Apply to]
info@ba-frm.de

[Links]
Web: **ba-frm.de**

- **Have a champion.**
  Check to see if a mutual contact can tell us about
  your strengths and recommend your business to us.

- **Solve a hard problem.**
  At Creathor Ventures, we're backing the creators
  of the future with big ambitions.

- **Have your numbers under control.**
  Make sure to have your numbers under control, and seek
  to bring on an additional team member early in case you
  lack the financial know-how.

- **Help us so we can help you.**
  Think in advance about how we'd be able to help
  you build your business and make it succeed.

Creathor Ventures

[Name]

[Elevator Pitch] *"We invest in the automation of industry and business as well as the personalization and digitalization of healthcare."*

[Sector] **Tech and life sciences**

[Description] Creathor Ventures was founded in 2003 as a successor to Technologieholding VC, which dates back to 1984. Today, Creathor manages over €230 million and has two offices, one in Bad Homburg and the other in Zurich. The firm's senior partners have successfully invested in the European startup ecosystem for over thirty years, providing funding to more than two hundred companies as lead or colead investors. More than twenty companies in Creathor's portfolio have been listed on international stock exchanges, and seven companies have reached a valuation of €1 billion or more. Several founders that received funding in the past have later invested in Creathor's funds themselves. Today, the fifteen-strong team supports over thirty tech and life science companies in development, growth and internationalization.

For its newest fund, Creathor Ventures is looking for ambitious founders who are solving hard problems with the help of data. Creathor Ventures' tech-investing team looks for startups and technologies that power the automation of industry and business, especially in the manufacturing, aerospace and automotive industries. Their life-sciences team takes a keen interest in startups and technologies that power the digitalization and personalization of healthcare, especially through diagnostics and devices. Digital health applications are of interest to both teams.

Initial investments from Creathor usually range between €500,000 and €2.5 million; however, Creathor does have the the capability (and willingness) to invest up to €10 million in the right startup. Notable Creathor portfolio companies include Blueprint Genetics, Doodle, HeyJobs, R3 Communications, Allthings, Phenex Pharmaceuticals, Wunderflats, Klara, Haja Networks and Imverse. The Creathor team strives to engage with and support founders early on; for example, through mentoring at several startup accelerators such as Techstars Berlin, Plug and Play Digital Health and Science4Life. They also welcome interested founders to contact them via introduction or directly through their website.

[Apply to] creathor.com/en/contact

[Links] Web: **creathor.com** Twitter: **@creathorventure**

229

- **Be part of a dedicated and compatible team.**
  Our key investment criteria are team, team and team!
  You should completely focus on the project success
  and fully understand and trust each other.

- **Demonstrate values.**
  Values such as respect, trust and integrity should
  be reflected in your management style.

- **Develop a disruptive market idea.**
  We invest in founders who are disrupting existing
  markets. We believe that small companies with fewer
  resources are able to successfully challenge established
  incumbent businesses.

- **Have fun.**
  Building up a business means an enormous personal
  commitment, which should be rewarded by fun
  and positivity among the team members and its
  business partners.

[Name]
Futury Venture Fonds

[Elevator Pitch]

"We're a newly established VC fund combining public money from the state of Hessen and from prominent business leaders and established corporates. Combining these partners, we provide our startups with a broad network allowing them to grow faster."

[Sector]

Tech-oriented solutions

[Description]

Futury Venture Fonds (FVF) is a newly established VC fund spin-off project from Futury, which is part of the nonprofit Werte-Stiftung (Values Foundation) in Germany. The Werte-Stiftung holds decades-long relationships with established medium and large companies and top managers, so Futury has dedicated themselves to giving startups and students the resources and networks to confidently and securely get their business idea up and running. FVF is a one-of-a-kind project in Germany, given that it pools private investments with public monies.

Futury Venture Fonds has a very broad network of entrepreneurs, business leaders, established corporates, universities, institutions and other investors. This extensive network helps startups to grow faster, develop new ideas and concepts, and rapidly scale their operations by identifying new business opportunities, opening the right doors and offering close-up coaching and advising.

Its fund volume amounts to €20 million and the state of Hessen (represented by the Hessen Ministry of Finance and the Hessen Ministry of Economics, Energy, Transport and Regional Development) provides half of the money, while private investors (including private individuals, family-run businesses, well-known firms and entrepreneurs) contribute the other half. Futury Venture Fonds generally invests between €100,000 and €500,000 per financing round, which can be anything from PoC-based seed capital to Series A financing. Furthermore, investments made are 50 percent dedicated to startups within the state of Hessen, with the other 50 percent provided throughout the rest of Germany. Together with their partner fund, BMH, Futury Venture Fonds is able to provide capital commitments to Hessen-based startups totaling between €2 million to €3 million. Additionally, their cooperation with e.ventures, a highly successful global VC firm, allows FVF's startups to scale up internationally and get exposure to global financing partners. They're open to all verticals, including engineering, software, internet, eHealth, mobility and logistics, and fintech, but want to see that there is a solid tech-related innovation in the business model.

[Apply to]

info@futuryvc.de

[Links]

Web: **futuryvc.de**

- **Have a balanced and complementary team.**
  As early-stage investors, we primarily invest in ideas and people. Your team should really represent your idea and passion for innovation.

- **Be technologically oriented.**
  Technology inspires us. What about you? Is your solution technologically advanced, and does it address the needs and problems of the financial service industry?

- **Solve a relevant use case for Commerzbank and Fintech in general.**
  We invest in startups that have a potential added value for Commerzbank and its customers.

- **Consider your market and competitors.**
  Your product or service should take into consideration the addressed market size, growth and timing, and be planned accordingly.

main Incubator

[Name]

[Elevator Pitch]
"We're the R&D Unit of Commerzbank Group and a strategic early-stage investor in technology driven startups."

[Sector]
Fintech, insurtech

[Description]
Established in 2014, main incubator is both the venture capital and research-and-development arm of the German Commerzbank Group. The main incubator VC has been set up to seek out entrepreneurs and innovators who are developing tech-oriented solutions that will not only benefit Commerzbank (and its endeavors to embrace a more digital future) but the bank's customers as well. Even though main incubator is primarily focused on solutions for the banking industry, there's a broad range of technologies that can be applied including blockchain, machine learning, AI, IoT, VR, robotics and even biometrics and wearables. The R&D prototyping department of main incubator is a means of being proactive in developing their own solutions in a similar range of technologies.

In the last four years, main incubator has invested in up to fifteen early-stage seed or Series A startups (fourteen portfolio, one exit) including Grover, Bilendo, Candis and Tillhub, and investments range from between €25,000 to €2 million with the sweet spot between €250,000 to €500,000 for an initial investment. There's no fixed model for how investments proceed, so main incubator is flexible in terms and criteria and welcomes co-investing with other VCs if there's a good fit.

Startups and founders are welcome to approach with their business idea or solution via the website, where it will be evaluated by the investment team and calls will be made if a potential fit is spotted. In addition, main incubator is very active in promoting a healthy fintech ecosystem via a monthly series of events called Between the Towers. These events serve to bring together those in the banking industry as well as investors, experts and media representatives, so startups are in the thick of the action for getting noticed and maybe making a deal.

[Apply to]
info@main-incubator.com

[Links]
Web: main-incubator.com Facebook: incubator.main Twitter: @mainincubator

directory

Startups

Africa GreenTec AG
Außenliegend 19
63512 Hainburg
africagreentec.com

CargoSteps
Kaiserstraße 61
60329 Frankfurt am Main
cargosteps.com

Clark Germany GmbH
Goethestraße 10
60313 Frankfurt
clark.de

Emma Matratzen GmbH
Wilhelm-Leuschner-Straße 78
Frankfurt am Main 60329
emma-matratze.de

FRAMEN GmbH
Liebigstraße 46
60323 Frankfurt
Myframen.com

Lizza GmbH
Dornhofstraße 31
63263 Neu-Isenburg
lizza.de

MINDS Medical
Eschersheimer Landstraße 1–3
60322 Frankfurt am Main
minds-medical.de

node.energy GmbH
Carl-von-Noorden-Platz 5
60596 Frankfurt am Main
Node.energy

Programs

**Accelerator Frankfurt
Mindspace Eurotheum**
Neue Mainzer Straße 66
60311 Frankfurt am Main
acceleratorfrankfurt.com

black chili GmbH
Otto-Meßmer-Straße 1
60314 Frankfurt am Main
blackchili.de

Goethe Unibator
Senckenberganlage 31
60325 Frankfurt am Main
goetheunibator.de

**GTEC - German Tech
Entrepreneurship Center**
Neue Rothofstraße 19
60313 Frankfurt
gtec.center

Merck KGaA
Frankfurter Straße 250
64293 Darmstadt Germany
innovationcenter.merckgroup.
com

PANDO. Ventures
Büdingenstraße 4–6
65183 Wiesbaden
pando-ventures.com

SAP SE
Dietmar-Hopp-Allee 16
69190 Walldorf
sap.com/next-gen

**Startup SAFARI
FrankfurtRheinMain**
Mindspace Frankfurt
Neue Mainzer Straße 66–68
60311 Frankfurt
frankfurt.startupsafari.com

**Startup Weekend
Mittelhessen**
Regionalmanagement
Mittelhessen
Georg-Schlosser-Straße 1
35390 Giessen
startup-weekend-
mittelhessen.de

TechQuartier
Platz der Einheit 2
60327 Frankfurt am Main
techquartier.com

Spaces

BEEHIVE
Mainzer Landstraße 33a
60329 Frankfurt
beehive.work

Co-Work & Play GmbH
Otto-Meßmer-Straße 1
60314 Frankfurt am Main
co-work-play.de

heimathafen Wiesbaden
Karlstraße 22
65185 Wiesbaden
heimathafen-wiesbaden.de

HUB31
Hilpertstraße 31
64295 Darmstadt
hub31.de

**Mindspace Frankfurt,
Eurotheum**
Eurotheum,Neue Mainzer
Straße 66–68
60311 Frankfurt
mindspace.me/frankfur

Social Impact Lab Frankfurt
Falkstraße 5
Frankfurt 60487
frankfurt.socialimpactlab.eu

WeWork Goetheplatz
Neue Rothofstraße 13–19
60313 Frankfurt HE
wework.com

Experts

BEITEN BURKHARDT
Mainzer Landstraße 36
60325 Frankfurt/Main
beiten-burkhardt.com/en

Deutsche Bank
Roßmarkt 18
60311 Frankfurt
deutsche-bank.de/startups

**FrankfurtRheinMain GmbH
International Marketing of
the Region**
Unterschweinstiege 8
60549 Frankfurt am Main
frm-united.com

Hessen Trade & Invest GmbH
Konradinerallee 9
65189 Wiesbaden
hessen-trade-and-invest.com

KPMG AG
The Square
60549 Frankfurt am Main
Germany
KPMG.de

Merck KGaA
Frankfurter Straße 250
64293 Darmstadt Germany
innovationcenter.merckgroup.
com

**Unternehmensgruppe
Nassauische Heimstätte /
Wohnstadt**
Schaumainkai 47
60596 Frankfurt
hubitation.de

R+V Versicherung AG
Raiffeisenplatz 1
65189 Wiesbaden
ruv.de

SAP Frankfurt
Frankfurter Straße 1
65760 Eschborn
sap.com/next-gen

Wirecard AG
Einsteinring 35
85609 Aschheim
wirecard.com

Founders

Acellere GmbH
Bockenheimer Landstraße 51
60325 Frankfurt a.M.
acellere.com
mygamma.io

Acomodeo
Am Salzhaus 4
60311 Frankfurt am Main,
Germany
acomodeo.com/en

Candylabs GmbH
Schwedlerstraße 6
60314 Frankfurt
candylabs.de

CoWorkPlay Eastside
Otto-Meßmer-Straße 1
60314 Frankfurt am Main
co-work-play.de

FastBill
Wildunger Straße 6
60487 Frankfurt am Main
fastbill.com

INGA
Hauptstraße 15
61231 Bad Nauheim
inga.one

Schools

**Frankfurt School of Finance
& Management gGmbH**
Adickesallee 32–34
60322 Frankfurt am Main
frankfurt-school.de

Goethe University Frankfurt
Theodor-W.-Adorno-Platz 1
60323 Frankfurt
uni-frankfurt.de

**RheinMain University of
Applied Sciences**
Kurt-Schumacher-Ring 18
65197 Wiesbaden, Germany
hs-rm.de/en

**Technische Universität
Darmstadt**
Schleiermacherstraße 10
Darmstadt 64283
tu-darmstadt.de

Investors

**Business Angels
FrankfurtRheinMain e.V.**
Börsenplatz 4,
60313 Frankfurt
ba-frm.de

Creathor Ventures
Schwedenpfad 24
61348 Bad Homburg
creathor.com

Futury Venture Fonds
Paul-Ehrlich-Straße 51
60596 Frankfurt am Main
Futuryvc.de

Main Incubator GmbH
Mainzer Landstraße 33a
60329 Frankfurt am Main
main-incubator.com

Startup Support

FinTech Headquarter
Münchener Straße 45
60329 Frankfurt am Main
fintechheadquarter.de

**Gründen & Wachsen
FRANKFURT BUSINESS
MEDIA GmbH – Der F.A.Z.-
Fachverlag**
Frankenallee 68–72
60327 Frankfurt am Main
gruenden-wachsen.de

Pitch Club AG
c/o Platz der Einheit 2
60327 Frankfurt am Main
thepitchclub.com

Media Partner

STATION
Mindspace Frankfurt
Neue Mainzer Straße 66–68
Frankfurt 60311
station-frankfurt.de

Event Partner

**THE ARTS+
Future of Culture Festival**
Frankfurter Buchmesse GmbH
Braubachstraße 16
60311 Frankfurt am Main
buchmesse.de

Accountants

Benefitax GmbH
Hanauer Landstraße 148a
60314 Frankfurt am Main
benefitax.de

GGV Partnerschaft mbB
WestendGate
Hamburger Allee 2-4
60486 Frankfurt am Main
gg-v.com/de

LÜBECK & Kollegen
Friedensstraße 11
60311 Frankfurt am Main
luebeckonline.com

WINHELLER Attorneys
at Law & Tax Advisors
Tower 185, Friedrich-Ebert-
Anlage 35-37
60327 Frankfurt am Main
winheller.com

Banks

Commerzbank
Aktiengesellschaft
Kaiserplatz
60311 Frankfurt am Main
commerzbank.de

Barclays Bank PLC
Taunustor 1
60310 Frankfurt am Main
barclays.de

Deutsche Bank AG
Taunusanlage 12
60325 Frankfurt am Main
Deutsche-bank.de

Frankfurter Sparkasse
Neue Mainzer Straße 47–53
60311 Frankfurt am Main
frankfurter-sparkasse.de

Helaba Landesbank
Hessen-Thüringen
Neue Mainzer Straße 52–58
60311 Frankfurt am Main
helaba.de

ING-DiBa AG
Theodor-Heuss-Allee 2
60486 Frankfurt am Main
ing-diba.de

Nassauische Sparkasse
Danziger Straße 12
65191 Wiesbaden
naspa.de

Postbank Deutsche
Postbank AG
Eckenheimer Landstraße 242
60320 Frankfurt am Main
postbank.de
Sparda-Bank Hessen eG
Osloer Straße 2
60327 Frankfurt am Main
sparda-hessen.de

Coffee Shops and Places with Wifi

Aniis - Raum für Kaffeekultur
Hanauer Landstraße 82
60314 Frankfurt am Main
aniis.de

Awake
Nibelungenplatz 3
60318 Frankfurt am Main
awake.coffee

Baltique
Heiligkreuzgasse 31
60313 Frankfurt am Main
baltique.de

Balzac Coffee
Schweizer Straße 43
60594 Frankfurt am Main
balzaccoffee.com

Café Mola
Diesterwegstraße 39
60594 Frankfurt am Main
mola-frankfurt.de

cafe sugar mama
Kurt-Schumacher-Straße 2
60311 Frankfurt am Main

The Holy Cross
Brewing Society
Fahrgasse 7
60311 Frankfurt am Main

Hoppenworth & Ploch
Friedberger Landstraße 86
60316 Frankfurt am Main
hoppenworth-ploch.de

MokkaTeeria
Heidestraße 149
60385 Frankfurt am Main
mokkateeria.de

OFOF Cafebar
Ludwigstraße 197
63067 Offenbach am Main
ofofcafebar.de

oheim
Oppenheimer Landstraße 48
60596 Frankfurt am Main
oheim.eu

Starbucks
An der Hauptwache 7
60313 Frankfurt am Main
starbucks.de

Expat Groups and Meetups

EXPAT in FFM -
Frankfurt am Main
facebook.com/groups/expat.
in.ffm.frankfurt.am.main

Frankfurt Expats Meetup
meetup.com/Frankfurt-Expats

Frankfurt Expat Talks
facebook.com/
groups/442228295883679

Internations Frankfurt
internations.org/frankfurt-
expats

Internationaler Stammtisch
RheinMain

Flats and Rentals

Immobilienscout24
immobilienscout24.de

Immonet
immonet.de

Immowelt
immowelt.de

Meine Stadt
meinestadt.de

Oflovesu
oflovesu.com

Salz und Brot
salzundbrot.com

Wohnungsboerse
wohnungsboerse.net

Wunderflats
wunderflats.de

Important Government Offices

Hessen Trade & Invest GmbH
Konradinerallee 9
65189 Wiesbaden
htai.de

Agentur für Arbeit Frankfurt am Main
Fischerfeldstraße 10–12
60311 Frankfurt am Main
arbeitsagentur.de

Bundesrepublik Deutschland – Finanzagentur GmbH
Lurgiallee 5
60439 Frankfurt am Main
deutsche-finanzagentur.de

Bundesamt für Wirtschaft und Ausfuhrkontrolle
Frankfurter Straße 29–35
65760 Eschborn
bafa.de

Handwerkskammer Frankfurt-Rhein-Main
Bockenheimer Landstraße 21
60325 Frankfurt am Main
hwk-rhein-main.de

Industrie- und Handelskammer Frankfurt am Main
Börsenplatz 4
60313 Frankfurt am Main
frankfurt-main.ihk.de

Wirtschaftsförderung Frankfurt – Frankfurt Economic Development – GmbH
Hanauer Landstraße 126-128
60314 Frankfurt am Main
frankfurt-business.net

Incubators and Accelerators

Accelerator Frankfurt GmbH
Neue Mainzer Straße 66
60311 Frankfurt am Main
acceleratorfrankfurt.com

blackprint PropTech Booster
Platz der Einheit 2
60327 Frankfurt am Main

Content Shift
Braubachstraße 16
60311 Frankfurt am Main
contentshift.de/en

E&Y Startup Initiative
start-up-initiative.ey.com/en

Gruendermaschine
Schleusenstraße 15–17
60327 Frankfurt am Main
gruendermaschine.com

Main-Incubator
Mainzer Landstrasse 33a
60329 Frankfurt am Main
main-incubator.com/en/home

PnP Fintech Europe
Platz der Einheit 2
60327 Frankfurt am Main

Unibator
SENCKENBERGANLAGE 31
JURIDICUM (5. OG)
60325 FRANKFURT AM MAIN
goetheunibator.de

Pando Ventures
Büdingenstraße 4–6
65183 Wiesbaden
pando-ventures.com

Insurance Companies

AGCS Frankfurt
Theodor-Stern-Kai 1
60596 Frankfurt am Main
agcs.allianz.com/services

Covomo Versicherungsvergleich GmbH
Rotfeder-Ring 5
60327 Frankfurt am Main
covomo.de

Finlex
FINLEX GmbH c/o WeWork
Neue Rothofstraße 13–19
60313 Frankfurt am Main
finlex.de/en

Language Schools

Berlitz Sprachschule
Kaiserstraße 6
60311 Frankfurt am Main
berlitz.de

eloquia Sprachschule
Kaiserstraße 10
60311 Frankfurt am Main
eloquia.com

Goethe-Institut Frankfurt
Sprachschule
Diesterwegplatz 72
60594 Frankfurt am Main
goethe.de/ins/de

Inlingua
Kaiserstraße 37
60329 Frankfurt am Main
inlingua-frankfurt.de

Perfect Lingua
Niedenau 39
60325 Frankfurt am Main
perfectlingua.com

Sprachschule Aktiv Frankfurt
Eschersheimer Landstraße 36
60322 Frankfurt am Main
sprachschule-aktiv.de

Sprachtreff
Alte Gasse 27–29
60313 Frankfurt am Main
sprachtreff.de

Sprachcaffe Sprachschule
Gartenstraße 6
60594 Frankfurt am Main
sprachcaffe.com

VHS
Sonnemannstraße 13
60314 Frankfurt am Main
vhs.frankfurt.de

Wall Street Institute
Kaiserstraße 44
60329 Frankfurt am Main
wallstreetenglish.de

Startup Events

12min.me Frankfurt
meetup.com/12minFFM

THE ARTS+ Future of Culture Festival
theartsplus.com

Bee for Startup Breakfast
meetup.com/BEE-for-Start-Up-Breakfast

Growthcon
growth-con.com

Entrepreneur University
entrepreneur-university.de

FinTech in and around Frankfurt
meetup.com/FinTech-in-and-around-Frankfurt

Fuckup Night
fuckupnightsfrankfurt.de

Gründerstammtisch / Founders Table FrankfurtRheinMain
meetup.com/Grunderstammtisch-Founders-Table-FrankfurtRheinMain

Open Coffee Club (OCC) Frankfurt
meetup.com/Open-Coffee-Club-OCC-Frankfurt

Pitch Club Frankfurt Startup Afterwork
meetup.com/Pitch-Club-Frankfurt-Startup-Afterwork

Rhein-Main Innovators
meetup.com/Darmstadt-InnovationM-Round-Table

RheinMainRocks
meetup.com/RheinMainRocks

Startup Grind Frankfurt
startupgrind.com/frankfurt

Startup Safari
frankfurt.startupsafari.com

Women Tech Makers Frankfurt
meetup.com/Women-Techmakers-Frankfurt_Rhein-Main

glossary

A

Accelerator
An organization or program that offers advice and resources to help small businesses grow

Acqui-hire
Buying out a company based on the skills of its staff rather than its service or product

Angel Investment
Outside funding with shared ownership equity

API
Application programming interface

ARR
Accounting (or average) rate of return: calculation generated from net income of the proposed capital investment

Artificial Intelligence
The simulation of human intelligence by computer systems; machines that are able to perform tasks normally carried out by humans

B

B2B
(Business-to-Business)
The exchange of services, information and/or products from a business to a business

B2C
(Business-to-Consumer)
The exchange of services, information and/or products from a business to a consumer

Blockchain
A digital, public collection of financial accounts in which transactions made in bitcoin or another cryptocurrency are recorded chronologically

BOM
(Bill of Materials)
A list of the parts or components required to build a product

Bootstrap
To self-fund, without outside investment

Bridge Loan
A loan taken out for a short-term period, typically between two weeks and three years, until long-term financing can be organized

Burn Rate
The amount of money a startup spends

Business Angel
An experienced entrepreneur or professional who provides starting or growth capital for promising startups

Business Model Canvas
A template that gives a coherent overview of the key drivers of a business in order to bring innovation into current or new business models

C

C-level
Chief position

Cap Table
An analysis of ownership stakes in a company

CMO
Chief marketing officer

Cold-Calling
The solicitation of potential customers who had no prior interaction with the solicitor

Convertible Note/Loan
A type of short-term debt often used by seed investors to delay establishing a valuation for the startup until a later round of funding or milestone

Coworking
A shared working environment

CPA
Cost per action

CPC
Cost per click

Cybersecurity
Technologies, processes and practices designed to protect against the criminal or unauthorized use of electronic data

D

Dealflow
Term for investors that refers to the rate at which they receive potential business deals

Deeptech
Companies founded on the discoveries or innovations of technologists and scientists

Diluting
A reduction in the ownership percentage of a share of stock due to new equity shares being issued

E

Elevator Pitch
A short summary used to quickly define a product or idea

Ethereum
A blockchain-based software platform and programming language that helps developers build and publish distributed applications

Exit
A way to transition the ownership of a company to another company

F

Fintech
Financial technology

Flex Desk
Shared desk in a space where coworkers are free to move around and sit wherever they like

I

Incubator
Facility established to nurture young startup firms during their first few months or years of development

Installed Base
The number of units of a certain type of product that have been sold and are actually being used

IP
(Intellectual Property) Property which is not tangible; the result of creativity, such as patents and copyrights

IPO
(Initial Public Offering) The first time a company's stock is offered for sale to the public

K

KPI
(Key Performance Indicator) A value that is measurable and demonstrates how effectively a company is achieving key business objectives

L

Later-Stage
More mature startups/companies

Lean
Refers to 'lean startup methodology;' the method proposed by Eric Ries in his book for developing businesses and startups through product development cycles

Lean LaunchPad
A methodology for entrepreneurs to test and develop business models based on inquiring with and learning from customers

M

M&A
(Mergers and Acquisitions) A merger is when two companies join to form a new company, while an acquisition is the purchase of one company by another where no new company is formed

MAU
Monthly active user

MVP
Minimum viable product

O

Opportunities Fund
Investment in companies or sectors in areas where growth opportunities are anticipated

P

P2P
(Peer-to-Peer) A network created when two or more PCs are connected and sharing resources without going through a separate server

Pitch Deck
A short version of a business plan presenting key figures generally to investors

PR-Kit (Press Kit)
Package of promotional materials, such as pictures, logos and descriptions of a company

Product-Market Fit
When a product has created significant customer value and its best target industries have been identified

Pro-market
A market economy/a capitalistic economy

S

SaaS
Software as a service

Scaleup
A company that has already validated its product in a market and is economically sustainable

Seed Funding
First round, small, early-stage investment from family members, friends, banks or an investor

Seed Investor
An investor focusing on the seed round

Seed Round
The first round of funding

Series A/B/C/D
The name of funding rounds that come after the seed stage

Shares
Units of ownership of a company that belong to a shareholder

Solopreneurs
A person who sets up and runs a business on their own and typically does not hire employees

Startup
Companies under three years old, in the growth stage and becoming profitable (if not already)

SVP
Senior Vice President

T

Term Sheet/Letter of Intent
The document between an investor and a startup including the conditions for financing (commonly non-binding)

U

Unicorn
A company, often in the tech or software sector, worth over US$1 billion

USP
Unique selling point

UX
(User experience design) The process of designing and improving user satisfaction with products so that they are useful, easy to use and pleasurable to interact with

V

VC
(Venture Capital) Financing from a pool of investors in a venture capital firm in return for equity

Vesting
Process that involves giving or earning a right to a present or future payment, benefit or asset

Z

Zebras
Companies which aim for sustainable prosperity and are powered by people who work together to create change beyond a positive financial return

STARTUP GUIDE TRONDHEIM — The Entrepreneur's Handbook
STARTUP GUIDE HAMBURG — The Entrepreneur's Handbook
STARTUP GUIDE LUXEMBOURG — The Entrepreneur's Handbook
STARTUP GUIDE VIENNA — The Entrepreneur's Handbook
STARTUP GUIDE TEL AVIV — The Entrepreneur's Handbook
STARTUP GUIDE MADRID — The Entrepreneur's Handbook
STARTUP GUIDE VALENCIA — The Entrepreneur's Handbook
STARTUP GUIDE COPENHAGEN — The Entrepreneur's Handbook
STARTUP GUIDE PARIS — The Entrepreneur's Handbook
STARTUP GUIDE REYKJAVIK — The Entrepreneur's Handbook
STARTUP GUIDE STOCKHOLM — The Entrepreneur's Handbook
STARTUP GUIDE MUNICH — The Entrepreneur's Handbook
STARTUP GUIDE FRANKFURT — The Entrepreneur's Handbook
STARTUP GUIDE ZURICH — The Entrepreneur's Handbook
STARTUP GUIDE LONDON — The Entrepreneur's Handbook
STARTUP GUIDE LISBON — The Entrepreneur's Handbook
STARTUP GUIDE NEW YORK — The Entrepreneur's Handbook
STARTUP GUIDE BERLIN — The Entrepreneur's Handbook
STARTUP GUIDE OSLO — The Entrepreneur's Handbook

→ startupguide.com Follow us

About the Guide

Based on traditional guidebooks that can be carried around everywhere, Startup Guide books help you navigate and connect with different startup scenes across the globe. Each book is packed with useful information, exciting entrepreneur stories and insightful interviews with local experts. We hope the book will become your trusted companion as you embark on a new (startup) journey. Today, Startup Guide books are in more than twenty different cities in Europe, the US and the Middle East, including Berlin, London, New York, Tel Aviv, Stockholm, Copenhagen, Vienna, Lisbon and Paris.

How we make the guides:

To ensure an accurate and trustworthy guide every time, we team up with locals partners that are established in their respective startup scene. We then ask the local community to nominate startups, coworking spaces, founders, schools, investors, incubators and established businesses to be featured through an online submission form. Based on the results, these submissions are narrowed down to the top hundred organizations and individuals. Next, the local advisory board – which is selected by our community partners and consists of key players in the local startup community – votes for the final selection, ensuring a balanced representation of industries and startup stories in each book. The local community partners then work in close collaboration with our international editorial and design team to help research, organize interviews with journalists as well as plan photoshoots with photographers. Finally, all content is reviewed, edited and put into the book's layout by the Startup Guide team in Berlin and Lisbon before going for print in Berlin.

Where to find us: The easiest way to get your hands on a Startup Guide book is to order it from our online shop: startupguide.com/shop

If you prefer to do things in real life, drop by one of the fine retailers listed on the stockists page on our website.

Want to become a stockist or suggest a store?

Get in touch here: sales@startupguide.com

STARTUP
GUIDE
STORE

The Startup Guide Stores

Whether it's sniffing freshly printed books or holding an innovative product, we're huge fans of physical experiences. That's why we have stores in Berlin and Lisbon and we're opening a third store in Copenhagen in November 2018. Not only do the stores showcase our books and a range of curated products, they're also our offices and a place for the community to come together and share wows and hows. But our stores wouldn't be possible without the help of Toyno, an experience design studio based in Lisbon. Visit their website here: toyno.com.

Lisbon:
Rua do Grilo 135, 1950-144 Lisboa
Mon-Fri: 10h-19h
+351 910 781 512
lisbon@startupguide.com

Berlin:
Waldemarstraße 38, 10999 Berlin
Mon-Fri: 10h-18h
+49 (0) 30 374 68 679
berlin@startupguide.com

Copenhagen:
Borgbjergsvej 1, 2450 København, Denmark
Mon-Fri: 10h-17h
+45 52 17 85 45
copenhagen@startupguide.com

#startupeverywhere

Startup Guide was founded by Sissel Hansen in 2014. As a publishing and media company, we produce guidebooks and online content to help entrepreneurs navigate and connect with different startup scenes across the globe. As the world of work changes, our mission is to guide, empower and inspire people to start their own business anywhere. Today, Startup Guide books are in more than 20 cities in Europe, the US and the Middle East, including Berlin, London, New York, Tel Aviv, Stockholm, Vienna, Lisbon and Paris. We also have three physical stores in Berlin, Lisbon and Copenhagen which double as offices for our 20-person team. Visit our website for more: startupguide.com

Want to get more info, be a partner or say hello?

Shoot us an email here info@startupguide.com

Join us and #startupeverywhere

Frankfurt Advisory Board

Ann Rosenberg
Senior Vice President,
Global Head of
SAP Next-Gen
SAP SE

Katrin Redmann
Innovation Lead DACH
& NextGen Innovation
Hub Lead SouthWest
Germany
SAP SE

Michael Nürnberg
Regional Director DACH
SAP University Alliances
& SAP Next-Gen
SAP SE

Jan Fiedler
Director Regional
Networks and
Cooperation
FrankfurtRheinMain
GmbH, International
Marketing of the Region

**Pedro Gonçalo
Mota Ferreira**
Managing Director
start zero

Sören Gahn
Head Startups@
Germany - Central
Region
Deutsche Bank AG

Robin Weninger
Managing Director
German Tech
Entrepreneurship Center
(GTEC)

Andreas Söntgerath
Creative Content
Strategist
schwarzwild
Kommunikation

Ram Shoham
Founder
Accelerator Frankfurt
GmbH

Joern Menninger
Founder and Host
Startuprad.io

Fabian Karau
Founder
Startupregionfrankurt

Céline Riemenschneider
Founding Partner
MI CEL Consulting

Carolin Wagner
Event Manager
Startup SAFARI
FrankfurtRheinMain
at candylabs GmbH
& Cofounder
STATION

**Paul Herwarth
von Bittenfeld**
Cofounder
STATION UG
(haftungsbeschränkt)

With thanks to our **Content Partners**

BEITEN BURKHARDT

Deutsche Bank ▨   hubitation

MERCK   wirecard

Our **Event Partner**

THE ARTS+

And our **Media Supporter**

STATION.
FrankfurtRheinMain

With thanks to our **Community Partner**

THEARTS+

of Future Culture Festival

THE/ARTS+

Event Partner / THE ARTS+ Future of Culture Festival

An international showroom for the future that brings together the creative minds and pioneers of the digital ecosystem; a festival with exciting micro-conferences that ask the basic questions – who, what and how – regarding the digital future; inspiring keynote talks by national and international speakers and exceptional performances; the ceremony for the Frankfurter Buchmesse Film Awards and the "Frankfurt Creative AI Conference": THE ARTS+ Future of Culture Festival is all this and more.

The festival sees itself as a link between cultural worlds and aims to create networks and synergies. It will take place for the fourth time as part of the Frankfurter Buchmesse, in Hall 4.1, from October 16 to 20, 2019.

THE ARTS+ is committed to shaping the digital and cultural ecosystem. Holger Volland, head of THE ARTS+ and vice president of the Frankfurter Buchmesse, says, "How does our understanding of culture and creativity change when it comes from machines? What will be our cultural legacy for future generations? Who will cultivate and curate it, and how? These are questions we will discuss at THE ARTS+ with politicians, museums, media companies, creatives, designers and pioneers from the technology and economic sector."

Just a few names on the excellent program in 2018 are Esther Wojcicki, Galit Ariel, JiaJia Fei, Frank Thelen, Tom Hillenbrand, Moon Ribas, Stein Olav Henrichsen, Harald Neidhardt, Marieke Reimann, Mark Mattingley-Scott, LIZZY "the human drum machine" and Maya Kodes, the virtual singer. In total, THE ARTS+ encompasses five days, seventy-one speakers, sixty events, fifty partners, sixty-seven exhibitors, three thousand conference and workshop visitors, 125,000 trade fair visitors, one virtual pop star, one cyborg, and one drum dress.

The upcoming program will be released shortly before the new festival starts. Stay updated via THE ARTS+ social media channels.

See you at #theartsplus19!

Media Partner / STATION

STATION is an online platform built to be the leading hub for startups and innovation in Frankfurt Rhine-Main, the largest economic area in central Germany. Besides Frankfurt, the region includes further innovation-driving metropolitan areas such as Wiesbaden, Mainz, Darmstadt and Offenbach.

STATION reaches out to all players in the ecosystem, encouraging and enabling founders, corporates, medium-sized companies, investors and job seekers to exchange ideas and cooperate with each other. Playing a pioneering role for Frankfurt Rhine-Main, STATION provides the regional ecosystem with relevant news and insights, the largest offering in startup events (including our own formats with Startup SAFARI FrankfurtRheinMain as a flagship), an innovation-focused job exchange, and a comprehensive range of databases facilitating everyone in the ecosystem who wishes to expand their network.

STATION grew out of Rhein Main Startups, the highest-reaching startup news portal for the area, and Startup SAFARI FrankfurtRheinMain, the largest decentralised networking event for the regional startup scene, consolidating their respective potential in content and events.

The people behind STATION are Daniel Putsche, founder and CEO of digital consulting firm Candylabs and initiator of Startup SAFARI FrankfurtRheinMain; Carolin Wagner, event specialist and managing director of Startup SAFARI FrankfurtRheinMain; and Paul Herwarth von Bittenfeld, initiator and operator of Rhein Main Startups.

[Links] Web: station-frankfurt.de Facebook: STATIONFRM Twitter @STATIONFRM

Startup Support / FinTech Headquarter

[Elevator Pitch]

"FinTech Headquarter ensures a quick and intense exchange between startups, founders, corporates, investors and legal institutions. With our network and online community, we bring together all the relevant players of the fintech ecosystem in Frankfurt Rhine-Main and all over Europe."

[Description]

FinTech Headquarter opened in 2015 as a coworking space for the fintech startup scene in Frankfurt. As a community enabler, it supports the fintech scene with its powerful network and cross-channel activities in Frankfurt and across Europe. FinTech Headquarter provides services such as networking events, coworking space, hangouts and meetups, and places a large focus on more specialized technologies such as blockchain and how they can be incorporated into new Fintech solutions. From the beginning, the strategy has been to strengthen the Frankfurt Rhine-Main business ecosphere and develop new fintech business models that can be scaled Europe-wide and then globally.

FinTech Headquarter was created to support founders and startups in developing and promoting their ideas so valuable connections can be made with experienced industry partners for advice, mentoring and financial support. It has four different membership options available: basic, standard, premium and unlimited, each offering different package benefits.

Its web service my.fintechheadquarter is a closed portal exclusive to members and can be used for digital networking and the exchange of ideas between startups, corporates, investors and legal via their own profile pages or the lively forums. The my.fintechheadquarter platform is also where startups and founders can create profiles with a three-minute video pitch to present their business ideas. Investors can browse through the profiles and rate the videos based on how interested they would be to make contact. Even if they don't want to get directly involved, the community of members willingly helps to evaluate the business ideas, and the startups benefit from solid industry knowledge. The FinTech Headquarter Loft in Frankfurt am Main offers a space for events and organizes regular networking events, such as the monthly Community HangOut.

[Links] Web: fintechheadquarter.de Facebook: fintechheadquarter Twitter: @FinTech_HQ

Startup Support
/ Gründen & Wachsen

[Elevator Pitch] *"We're a community that pursues the goal of strengthening the innovative power of founders and growth companies through events, competitions, coaching, publications, and networks, making them accessible to the general public and offering founders direct assistance."*

[Description] The Gründen & Wachsen Community of the F.A.Z.-Fachverlag focuses on helping founders and companies develop through its series of programs, workshops, events and other community projects. Initiatives include BEST EXCELLENCE, a program that supports founders and startups at all stages of development using a practice-oriented approach to reflect the different phases of starting a business; and Gründerflirt (FounderFlirt), which helps entrepreneurs who have an idea but still require developers or business and sales knowledge. Gründerflirt gives founders, startups and re-starters the chance to implement their startup idea in a team, expand their team or contribute their expertise to a startup company.

"Gründen, Förden, Wachsen" is the main event within the Global Entrepreneurship Week Germany. It offers founder stories, workshops, exchange lounges and discussions with experts. Another initiative, the STEP Award competition, recognizes innovative and high-growth companies from Germany, Austria, and Switzerland and helps them take their first steps into the ecosystem. Since 2006, the competition has been aimed primarily at B2B growth companies in scientific sectors. The Unternehmensnachfolge (Business Succession) initiative tackles the increasing generational change in German companies. Its purpose is to initiate and support smooth transfer processes and educate on the subject of "corporate succession."

Through a variety of events, Gründen & Wachsen offers the opportunity to not only receive information and individual advice from qualified experts but also to get to know potential "transferers" or "transferees" and to exchange ideas via personal conversations. In addition, Gründen & Wachsen cooperates with Für-Gründer.de, a platform that offers tons of written resources covering a variety of topics. The project also sets startups up with their partners and offers mentoring.

Startup Support / Pitch Club

[Elevator Pitch]

"At Pitch Club, we match innovative, early-stage startups with experienced investors, while at Pitch Club Developer Edition, we match highly skilled software developers with companies (MNCs, SMEs & startups)."

[Description]

Since 2014, Pitch Club and their unique format has made them Rhine-Main's number-one pitch event, with over 160 startups and 500 investors attending. Pitch Club hosts two different events: the traditional Pitch Club gives young, innovative early-stage startups the possibility to present their business model in front of experienced investors, and the Pitch Club Developer Edition, which started in 2017, has been adapted into a recruitment event where companies, CTOs and lead developers present themselves and the jobs they have on offer in front of preselected software developers.

Pitch Club was initiated with the idea of developing the Frankfurt Rhine-Main's startup scene and pivoting away from what organizers have considered very fragmented to a solid, strong and inclusive ecosystem for startups, investors and corporates. Prior to the event, organizers review up to one hundred applications and make a shortlist of twenty startups that pique their interest. After a phone interview with each candidate, the final group of ten is selected. Key criteria for making the final list are market potential, first proof of concept and a demonstrated ability to roll out and execute a solid business model. At the Pitch Club events, each startup gets a six-minute pitch slot to wow the crowd, followed by the chance to have detailed one-on-ones with investors and corporate representatives in attendance. The events always conclude with an informal afterwork party with food and drinks.

In addition to events, Pitch Club also offers services for startups, investors and corporates (such as the scouting and sourcing of startups for corporates and investors) and varied workshops. They are in a great position to make solid connections, having forged strong partnerships with the likes of TechQuartier, Goethe Unibator, Climate KIC, Business Angels network, Code_n, Startplatz, many corporates and initiatives like Startup Grind.

[Links]   Web: **thepitchclub.com** Facebook: **thepitchclub** Twitter: **@PitchClubFFM**

WHERE NEXT?